Munbaz II
and other
Mitzvah Heroes

BOOKS BY DANNY SIEGEL

Mitzvahs	1980 -	ANGELS*
	1982 -	GYM SHOES AND IRISES* (Personalized Tzedakah)
	1987 -	GYM SHOES AND IRISES - BOOK TWO*
	1988 -	MUNBAZ II AND OTHER MITZVAH HEROES
	1989 -	FAMILY REUNION: Making Peace in the Jewish Community
	1990 -	MITZVAHS
	1993 -	AFTER THE RAIN: The Book of Mitzvah Power for Adults and Teens
For Children	1993 -	TELL ME A MITZVAH *(Published by Kar-Ben Copies)*
	1993 -	THE HUMONGOUS PUSHKA IN THE SKY
Humor	1982 -	THE UNORTHODOX BOOK OF JEWISH RECORDS AND LISTS (With Allan Gould)
Poetry	1969 -	SOULSTONED*
	1976 -	AND GOD BRAIDED EVE'S HAIR*
	1978 -	BETWEEN DUST AND DANCE*
	1980 -	NINE ENTERED PARADISE ALIVE*
	1983 -	UNLOCKED DOORS (An Anthology)
	1985 -	THE GARDEN: Where Wolves and Lions Do No Harm to the Sheep and the Deer
	1985 -	THE LORD IS A WHISPER AT MIDNIGHT (Psalms and Prayers)
	1986 -	BEFORE OUR VERY EYES Readings for a Journey Through Israel
	1991 -	THE MEADOW BEYOND THE MEADOW
	1992 -	A HEARING HEART
Midrash and Halachah	1983 -	WHERE HEAVEN AND EARTH TOUCH (Book One)*
	1984 -	WHERE HEAVEN AND EARTH TOUCH (Book Two)*
	1985 -	WHERE HEAVEN AND EARTH TOUCH (Book Three)*
	1985 -	WHERE HEAVEN AND EARTH TOUCH SOURCE BOOK (Selected Hebrew and Aramaic Sources)
	1988 -	WHERE HEAVEN AND EARTH TOUCH (Combined Volumes: Book One, Two and Three)
	1989 -	WHERE HEAVEN AND EARTH TOUCH (Combined Volumes) in Hardbound Edition

*Out of print

Danny Siegel

Munbaz II
AND OTHER
Mitzvah Heroes

THE TOWN HOUSE PRESS
Pittsboro, North Carolina

I with to express my gratitude to the following people who helped me write this book:

To Phyllis Greene, who gave me the idea to write this book.

To my good friend, Garth Potts, who wrote the section on sports heroes, and who has instructed me in many ways about how Torah and Mitzvahs interweave with real life.

To my brother, Stan, for teaching me how to use the Macintosh and for pulling me through the many crises that arise from relating to even the most marvellous machines.

To my editor, Edyth Siegel (also known as ''Mom''). All those years as a journalist paid off. She patiently read and re-read the manuscript and smoothed the style. If the book is readable, it is because of Mom.

To Amy Ripps for not only helping with the manuscript but also for assisting in my Ziv Tzedakah Fund work when there simply would not have been enough time to do both the book and the Ziv activities.

To Lorraine Mackler for assisting in the proofreading of the manuscript.

Third Printing, 1994
Cover by Fran Schultzberg

Photographs of Myriam Mendilow and Hadassah and Her Gang
        by Linda S. Kantor.
Photograph of The Rabbanit Kapach by Jay Wolke.
Photograph of the author by Craig Terkowitz of the Baltimore Jewish Times.

Library of Congess Catalogue Card Number: 88-50923
International Standard Book Number: 0-940653-13-3

For ordering:
The Town House Press
552 Weathersfield, Pittsboro NC 27312

For my friends
Jack Gruenberg and Marc Sternfeld

TABLE OF CONTENTS

TERMINOLOGY

There are three essential Hebrew words I use many times in this book. They appear in different contexts, along with certain grammatical variations. It is important for the reader to understand from the very beginning how I am using the terms.

"Tzedakah" is variously translated as "Righteousness" or "Doing the Right Thing". It also means "Using one's own resources to bring fairness, equity, and decency into the lives of others". Tzedakah is the Jewish way of giving, i.e., giving out of a sense of justice and doing the right thing.

"Tzedek" means "Justice", and it is the motivating force for Tzedakah acts. A person performs an act of Tzedakah because he or she senses that there is something wrong in the world, and that person determines to set things right once again through an act of Tzedakah.

"Tzaddik" (masculine form) and "Tzadeket" (feminine) are variant forms of the same Hebrew root, and they signify someone who personifies by his or her actions and lifestyle the principles of Tzedakah and Tzedek. "Tzaddik" and "Tzadeket" range in meaning from "A Righteous Person", to "One who personifies generosity", to "One who does the right thing", to "One who embodies the principles of Justice" and, finally, to "A good person to the highest degree".

"Mitzvahs" means "Doing good things". In the broadest traditional Jewish sense of the word, "Mitzvahs" can mean "commandments from God", or "divine instructions on how to live a good life". Mitzvahs extend into every aspect of daily Jewish life; they include the laws of keeping Kosher, the Sabbath and holidays, and many other acts. In this book, I use "Mitzvah" in the more restricted and colloquial sense of "A good act". Thus, a Mitzvah Hero is one who lives a life suffused with good works, and who is admirable for all the good things he or she does.

INTRODUCTION

There is something very admirable and attractive about the people I am about to describe. They are, on the one hand, astounding and stunning, and, on the other hand, very human like ourselves.

For more than a dozen years I have been obsessed with the Mitzvah of Tzedakah, exploring the Jewish mode of giving from many different perspectives. I have tried to get the "feel" of Tzedakah by establishing a non-profit organization called Ziv Tzedakah Fund. Because of generous contributions from friends and strangers alike, I have had the privilege of channeling nearly half a million dollars to various Mitzvah heroes and Tzedakah projects. In addition, I have examined some of the traditional Jewish texts about this Mitzvah, have taught some of the same texts, and have spent many hours thinking about the essences of Tzedakah.

Recently, though, my thoughts have taken a specific turn: I have focused my primary studies on the Real Life Living of the Mitzvah, i.e., the way Tzedakah is personified and acted out in the real world. Inevitably, this has led me to Giants and Heroes and Role Models and Tzaddikim — whatever you wish to call them. To some extent it has forced me to put the abstracts of Tzedakah into the background. I am still interested, of course, in the texture and variations of the Mitzvah, the way it integrates into the very stuff of God's plan as portrayed in the Bible and expounded in the Talmud. On a highly theoretical level, Tzedakah is embedded in the world; it is in The Nature of Things, and waits to be actualized by human beings in day-to-day acts. But that is all abstract theology and philosophy, a difficult subject. It is no doubt a fruitful topic to pursue, but it is not my primary concern at the moment.

So, of late, I have turned to the Mitzvah heroes, those captivating people who draw you into their circle so powerfully and yet, more often than not, so gently. My purpose in recording some aspects of their lives and Mitzvah work is a most practical one: I would like people to read this book and say, "Oh, I must meet these people, work with them, do something." I want my readers to meet the Heroes and listen to them and ask them questions: *How* did you start? *Why* did you start? *What* keeps you going? *How much* does this interfere with the rest of your life? *Where* do you get the time and energy and faith to do so much? *How* can *I* do some of this?

As I write this introduction I recall an afternoon lecture in Miami. I had just shown a short videotape of Trevor Ferrell at work. (He's "The Kid" in Philadelphia who feeds homeless people.) I asked the group what it was exactly about Trevor that impressed them and appealed to them. One person responded, "He's doing something!"

That is the story of every one of these people. What they all have in common is this: instead of whining or sulking or railing against The Evils of The

World, they set out to do something to change things, to alter-for-the-good their immediate surroundings, the entire world, or both.

So join me as I describe the lives of some of the people I have met along the way, and some of the others I have yet to meet, but have read about and hope to meet sometime soon.

I wish you the same joy and uplift I have felt in these encounters.

Danny Siegel
May, 1988

JANET MARCHESE

It all began on a rainy night about eleven years ago.

That sounds like an opening sentence for many bad novels, but this story *did* begin about eleven years ago on a rainy night. It is the story of Janet Marchese, and it is all about babies.

As with so many of the Mitzvah heroes I have met, I first heard about Janet through stories my friends told me, or through articles they sent me from some newspaper or magazine. I always read the articles and then either file them or take them with me to my speaking engagements. I often say to myself, "If I am in the neighborhood, I'll try to meet X or Y."

With Janet, it took three tries. The first time it didn't work out for one reason or another. The second time her father-in-law was sick. Twice was enough, almost; I nearly removed her from my priority list of "Angels to Visit".

But I was due to make one more trip up to Westchester for a speaking engagement, one more chance this year, and I asked my friend Jack Gruenberg to try to arrange a get-together at Janet's house, which he did.

Then, as has happened so often in my life, my life changed rhythm and depth and texture — all in the course of a few hours of conversation. By the time our first meeting was over, I understood the ecstasies art connoisseurs and devotees of good music feel when viewing a masterpiece or hearing a great symphony performed with wisdom and finesse. And yet, this encounter with Janet was something more: *those* experiences are Art, in the world of aesthetics....this was *Life*.

THE 1,200 BABIES

No more delay.

Janet Marchese (pronounced Mar-Kay-Zee) has a network, a delicate interweaving of people's lives more vast than any I am aware of of its kind. She hears of people who give birth to children with Down's Syndrome and other disabilities who might not want to keep them. There are many reasons. And on the other end of the network, she knows families that want to adopt these babies. Janet links all of them together.

That's 1,200 babies in about 11 years, or one about every 3 1/3 days for more than a decade. I once asked her on the phone if a week ever goes by without a call. "Not in a *long* time!" she answered. Even on my 4th try, when I wanted to see her again over Passover, things didn't work out. She had to visit five families that week, five families to talk to. That's what Janet does. (And four of the families concluded after she visited them that they did, indeed, want to keep the children.) She never condemns the parents if they don't want to keep the child, and she never tries to swing them to keeping one if they have made up their mind. But many of the parents are simply uncertain, even confused as to what to do, and that is where Janet comes in.

I have read books like *Playing God in the Nursery* and other personal accounts of the agonizing decisions that go with giving birth to and raising special children....both the sublime tales and the stories of frustration, break-up and failure. None of these people, least of all Janet, would say this kind of work or life is easy. That's naive and right out of Hollywood. But Janet's contention is that the parents are entitled to a fair, full picture of the possibilities. Naturally enough, tension often runs high, because these decisions are usually made in the first few hours or days of the baby's life. But she neither condemns nor criticizes the decisions of the parents.

THE RAINY NIGHT

So much goes along with Janet's story, so many ideas, adjuncts, corollaries, implications. My mind was full after our first meeting; it continued to fill and flow and push to the limits whenever I would speak of her.

Circuits start connecting at frantic speed all over my brain when I picture myself sitting in her kitchen and having coffee with her and my friend Jack. Electricity surges everywhere in my head. When that kitchen and the coffee and

Janet and T.J. Marchese at their home in White Plains, New York.

conversation come to mind, so many other things that wear my life down become insignificant: the money people owe me, the rush to continue establishing my career on firm foundations, whether or not I will ever fix the tail light on my car, whether or not I'll find the time to buy two white shirts so the new suits will co-ordinate perfectly with the shoes and ties. A minor incident illustrates my point, i.e., how with Janet you are in a different realm — like Calculus-and-beyond rather than multiplication tables: while talking with Janet in the kitchen, naturally enough the family dog came in from roaming around outside. He is a *big*, scruffy dog, and *I* am generally afraid of dogs. But since we are in the *Marchese's* home, he turns out to be very gentle. He is appropriately named "Bear", and, as one would expect by now, he was a hound that someone was going to put to sleep and Janet and the family saved him from destruction. *That's* what I have come to know as the normal course of events with people like Janet and her family.

And so, it was a rainy night, about eleven years ago. Janet and her husband, Louis, were waiting for some foster parents to drop off a baby they would watch for a week while the foster parents went on vacation. The Marcheses were in the process of adopting two Korean children and had already received approval from the adoption agency. (They already had two of their own.) During this waiting period, the agency called and asked them to babysit this foster child. I don't know what originally led the Marcheses to want to adopt two children from overseas. They had their reasons, and they were deemed fit by the appropriate authorities, and this is how they came to be waiting (for the kids from overseas) when the other, most fortuitous phonecall came.

It was a rainy night. A car pulled into the driveway. The foster parents came to the door stinking of alcohol. The baby was not properly wrapped up against the weather and Janet and Louis took in the baby and knew soon, very soon, that they would not give up this baby, but would adopt it. They did: he is T.J. Marchese, and he has Down's Syndrome.

Now this is where the story gets a little muddled, and I do not remember all the details: there's something about another couple, somewhere in Connecticut, waiting to adopt a child that had special needs. Janet remembered them, and heard from somewhere else that some couple in some other place did not think they could keep their newborn child with Down's, and she linked them up. That is — approximately — how it all began, 1,200 babies ago.

T.J. is now eleven, and I don't suppose he is any more or less amazing than the people with an extra chromosome that I have met or seen on TV in the Special Olympics or read about in one of the many articles people send me or I find on my own. Neither Janet nor I believe the lines you hear like "Special kids always get special parents" or "Kids with Down's always have such pleasant personalities" or anything like that, but T.J. seems to be a decent kid. If I were biased, I would say, "He seems a hell of a lot nicer than many kids I have met who have normal chromosomes", but that's patronizing. And we're certainly not going to say "He *suffers* from Down's", though I just saw that phrase in a recent edition of *People*

Magazine today while waiting to get my eyes checked at the optometrist's. He's just a "plain old kid", one of 5 Marchese children whose Dad happens to be a policeman who's in charge of all the plumbing in New York City police facilities and whose Mom works as a part-time waitress, and on the side happens to help match-up families who want to adopt special kids with others who cannot manage such a situation.

So we'll leave T.J. out of this.

This is *Janet's* story.

JANET HERSELF

I happen to like Janet. A lot. That's not always the situation when you meet the subject of amazing human stories. Though on a lesser scale, I, personally, à la Charles Kuralt, like to look for these people on TV, in the movies, in the papers and magazines, and I have a growing number of people around the country who send me interesting articles about them. What I have learned is that there *are* quite a few of the amazing people around, but some of them are a little hard to deal with, either because they are such fanatics for Mitzvahs they cannot tolerate hardheartedness or apathy, or because they are so high-powered, the people who come into their circle can't keep up with them and a lot of friction results. This is definitely not the case with Janet.

She sets you very much at ease, right away. I think that's probably a result of two things: the "natural touch" and the fact that, since she has been involved in over 1,000 family situations on one end and another more-than-1,000 on the other, she's probably had to know how to make people relax, quickly.

As to the "natural touch" part of it....even after a dozen years of looking into this phenomenon of Mitzvah heroes, I still can't determine if some people are born with it or not. But wherever and whenever and however Janet got it, she's got it.

She's lively, enormously natural and unpretentious. She is tall, though it isn't important if she is tall or short (though I have met both types), physically attractive or dumpy (though I have seen and talked to both kinds), un-college-educated or a laureate with two PhD's or more (though I have met both; though Janet never went to college, but I am *not* implying that *not* having a college education makes you better prepared for this Grandeur of the Soul). She is inordinately energetic, a characteristic common to many of the Heroes, and a red-flag warning to students and confederates of theirs that, if their metabolism is not up to that of the Hero or Heroine, they should beware, and gauge their own energy levels, lest, with all good intentions, they burn themselves up.

Somewhere along the way, I forgot to ask Janet if she is doing this because she is religious. Now I don't know if she is a Catholic or a Protestant; neither do I know whether or not she is a good or bad Christian in the ritual sense of the term, nor whether or not Christianity as she personifies it plays any role at all in her work. It is none of my business, though for me, personally, this is not always an irrelevant question. Since I am a Jewish educator who would like to see religious teachings move its followers into this realm of making religion live on an intense human level, I *am* generally curious about this issue. Reviewing in my mind a range of Heroes I have met, there are both kinds: those whose starting point is their religious belief, and others who seem to grasp hold of Tzedakah and Tzedek — Doing the Right Thing — as simply a part of what being human means. The end result is the same: beneficiaries benefit....for Janet, babies with limitations of some sort; for others, the poor and hungry and homeless or the addicted or lonely or refugees or migrant workers or people near death — whomever.

After I finish this book, I might ask Janet about her Christian leanings. Maybe. For now, as a poet, I would prefer to picture someone like Janet as a Baal Shem Tov kind of person. The Baal Shem Tov, according to our best accounts, was a child-like kind of person who revolutionized Judaism in Eastern Europe a couple of centuries ago. The Chassidic movement began with this person who was filled with wonder, who loved the forests and the rest of God's world and most of all, children. He was, in the best sense of the word, a simple person, what we would call in Hebrew "Tam" or "Tamim".

If Janet is a churchgoer, I would like to picture her as one who sits in the pews and admires the stained glass windows in a kind of modest reverie; who listens to the choir and is swept away not so much for the content of the hymn or sacred text as for the sheer beauty and miracle of the human voice and how it raises the soul to more sublime realms, just as I would imagine her standing silently on a starry, starry night, admiring the awesome heavens but drawing no particularly eloquent or profound theological conclusions. Just as I do not know whether or not she philosophizes about her work with the babies and their families, so, too, I have no sense of whether or not she reflects on the mysteries and intricate systems of whatever religious affiliation she might have. That's just me, the poet, musing, and whether or not any of it is true will only be determined after the book has been published.

Janet has no apparent affectations, and I would assume that, aside from normal family situations when she has to shout at the kids about this or that, or other familial tensions...I would suggest that there are probably plenty of people out there who would like to adopt her for a mother. And, as with all mothers, no one would imply that Janet is perfect. She's just less scarred, irritating and bothersome than some other mothers we might have met in our travels. If you want strain and tension, shoutings and an uncomfortable feeling in the household air, go elsewhere.

JANET AND HER NETWORK: HEROICS

It's this network of people that keeps coming to mind, this thing she fell into 11 years ago. It has grown and grown and grown, and you have to start wondering how it is that so many people don't know about such a network — particularly the side of it where there are so many families who want to adopt kids with special characteristics who might make special demands (and ever-so-frequently give special rewards) in the process of raising them. I can't figure it out, since we hear so much about what is supposed to be the whole range of societal treatment of children with disabilities: the scandals of "warehousing" and the abuses in institutions and the normalcy of mainstreaming and the now-and-again triumphs of individuals with disabilities getting fine jobs or running their own companies or getting their doctorates and winning awards or whatever. With all this other stuff flying around, how can we not have known at all about Janet's network. Indeed, I was astonished to learn that whenever we hear on the news or read about people who do not want to continue medical treatment of "special kids" — whenever we hear that — we should be aware of the fact that there is *always* some family that is ready to adopt and raise the child. That includes infants and children with the most severe disabilities. How is it that we don't hear so frequently about these adopting families?

Furthermore, since many people ask me to check out various places and people to which they might want to contribute their money, I am always required to investigate the hard facts: in this particular case, was Janet some sort of fanatic or lunatic? Was she mopping up on fees? Was she dealing in black-market babies? Now that I look back on the initial meeting with Janet, it seems silly and embarrassing and outrageous that I should have been suspicious at all...but still I had to check. This is the detective part of Tzedakah work. It is sometimes unpleasant and not really part of my nature, but it is a necessary part of the work.

She is who she is: too good to be true, one might say. But it is a fact: there *are* apparently a number of these people around who, though they sound too good to be true, really are all that they are made out to be. Cynics and critics may say I exaggerate, but I suspect they haven't been around The Giants as much as I have, and certainly not as much as another of my heroes, Charles Kuralt, whose wanderings among the Giants I follow frequently. *He*, at least, thinks these people are as true as they seem to be, and I am comforted that he and I are on the same side.

Thus, for the Student of Heroes, it is comforting to know that there are angels of every variety (wouldn't it have been nice if her name had been "Angela"?) walking among us human beings, enlightening and touching us, if we but make the effort to meet them and be enlightened and touched.

There is an additional issue: Why would it be that more people don't go out of their way to meet these people, these Heroes?

One reason is a possible feeling of guilt and inadequacy: the heroes are doing so much, and *I* am doing so little — it strikes a little to heavily in the gut. Personal contact can make the contrast too painful. One defense for this is admiring the Heroes so much that people can safely distance yourself and *not* have to say, "I would like to be like that, too — to whatever extent possible. I will *do* something. I *will* do something."

On the other hand, meeting Janets and others like her could be viewed as an opportunity, a chance to focus on what people can be if they choose to exceed their previously-held image of themselves. They can throw out all their self-growth books and booklets and newsletters and just get down to being themselves in the highest sense. I see this choice as a most fulfilling one for many people.

Once upon a time Dan Rather came to the house to interview Janet, trailing, as Janet describes it, blocks and blocks of trucks with all kinds of sophisticated electronics equipment. Rather insisted that he had only such-and-such amount of time, since he had a meeting early that afternoon. As the hour approached for his other meeting, he took off his jacket, loosened his tie, took some more coffee, and just sat and listened, long past his appointed hour of meeting whatever other person was on the day's schedule.

When Jack and I (lesser mortals, to be sure) went to meet Janet, we did the same, shoving other less consequential things aside, as you no doubt will also do when you go to meet her.

SALARY

Janet makes no money from her adoption project. Last year she had phone bills of $10,000, and only recently got a grant from the Kennedy Foundation and some additional money from another like-minded group. She supports her work from her husband Louis's salary, her part-time waitressing, and from her dolls.

Janet's dolls.

You notice them when you walk into the house — they are scattered everywhere: hand-made dolls, antique dolls, fancy dolls, dolls worth $75, $100, $500, $800, many of them donated to her or given at cost, so she can support her "habit". They are all over the place: on couches, windowsills, the mantelpiece. The Marchese kids must think that this is the most magical household in the world with all those dolls.

But, no, she doesn't get a salary for all this.

(Though there *are* other forms of compensation: a dozen kids have been named for Janet, one for Louis, one for TJ, and a few others for other members of the family.)

A FOOTNOTE

The first article I read about Janet said she had helped place 300 babies in adoptive homes; that is the figure that I mentioned in my book *Gym Shoes and Irises: Book Two*. Then, as I was about to have a second printing run on the book, I called her friend, Emily Kingsley, who put the figure at "more than 1,000".

Now, at the time of a third printing, I called Janet again (October 1993) and she said, "more than 3,000."

They come from every kind of home: rich, poor, intellectual, uneducated, religious, not religious, young or old parents, Jewish and not Jewish.

Of the more than 3,000 babies given up to adoption, about half are Jewish. Janet has recently found a fourth Jewish home to adopt one of these infants with special needs.

Janet Marchese, 56 Midchester Ave., White Plains NY 10606, 914-428-1236.

REFLECTIONS I

One of my prize possessions in a gift from my mother. I asked her for it.

It is a photograph of a group of newspaper reporters standing with Eleanor Roosevelt outside some mansion in New Jersey. The group had just interviewed the First Lady, and Mom is standing to Mrs. Roosevelt's right. The picture was taken some time in the late Thirties when my mother was working for the Asbury Park Press.

It was a great day for my mother. She admired Mrs. Roosevelt, read her column, "My Day", regularly, and followed her humanitarian activities wherever they took her. I even recall the pain in my mother's voice when, shortly after Mrs. Roosevelt died, she spoke of how much the woman had suffered from her final bouts with disease.

Inevitably when I ask my audiences about Heroes, I say, "I am thinking of three women, two Jewish and one not Jewish, who were heroic figures in my mother's day. Who are they?" And, just as inevitably, the answers are Mrs. Roosevelt, Henrietta Szold (the founder of Hadassah), and Golda Meir. Always those three.

As it happens, my mother also had the opportunity to meet Miss Szold, in Atlantic City, also in the late Thirties. It was the last Hadassah Convention that Henrietta Szold attended.

I just now called Mom, to see if she had also met Golda Meir. Indeed she did, once in Jerusalem when Golda was Prime Minister, and one other time....in 1947 or so, at a Zionist gathering in Washington. She and my Aunt Anna heard her and Moshe Sharett (then Shertok) at some rally.

I know it would be silly to ask my mother if she wanted to be like these three people "when she grew up". I know the answer would be Yes.

Eleanor Roosevelt and reporters in Middletown, New Jersey, in late 1930's. The author's mother, Edythe Siegel, is to Mrs. Roosevelt's immediate right.

HADASSAH LEVI

Hadassah Levi is raising 38 children with Down's Syndrome, a genetically-based irregularity that results from the presence of an extra chromosome. Some children are more severely affected, some less so, though all have some degree of retardation. However, it is improper to say, "This child (or this person) *suffers* from Down's Syndrome." More appropriately, the phrase is, "The child (or person) *has* Down's Syndrome."

The fact that Hadassah is raising thirty-eight children with this anomaly should be enough to gain her entry into a multitude of halls of fame. Many such children with Down's Syndrome are rejected by society and individuals within that society, but she loves them, accepts them, and *always* relates to them as unique human beings. Extra energies are needed to raise the children because they have special needs. And all Hadassah wants is to be left alone so she can help her children grow up, receive a decent education, and live the full, good life. For some reason, though, people don't want to leave her alone: near and faraway neighbors, mean-spirited bureaucrats, and many total strangers with apparently nothing better to do than to bring misery and hardship to her and her kids have all made her struggle a most agonizing trial.

The history of Hadassah's Kids is relatively simple, and possibly the only simple thing about her story. About fifteen years ago she had a place called Ma'on HaYeled, a day-care center for retarded children up through their teens in a suburb near Tel Aviv called Ramat Gan.

How I got to meet her is a little more roundabout: I was spending a year in Jerusalem, from August, 1973 to August, 1974. I was writing more poetry then and thought a year of writing, studying on my own, and wandering around Jerusalem and Israel would be a good theme-setting experience for the rest of my life. I had a nice apartment, a good view, and, fortunately, a library left behind by the professor whose place I had: Talmuds, Biblical materials, Judaica on a grand scale.

In August of that year I watched the conclusion of the annual Tze'adah, a three-day march of thousands of people, Israelis and foreigners of all ages who camped out somewhere in Israel and walked their way into Jerusalem. Though it is almost fifteen years ago, I can not only see the proud looks on the faces of the thousands who participated, I can remember ever-so-clearly the good feelings all in the air. Here was a Fun Thing in Israel: pure, unoppressive joy, unattached to a long history of wars and pogroms and infiltrators and sieges. I love simplicity, and the simplicity of the idea (like the circus or a clown visiting children in a hospital) suffused me with a joy mixed with purity that is achievable only on rare occasions in one's lifetime. I loved it, and when I take my photographs out from the Tze'adah of 1973, I can immediately summon up those feelings.

A month later it was war. Yom Kippur afternoon and long into the night after the Fast of Repentance, army vehicles of every size and type snaked their way down Herzog Street, up past the big hill near the Holy Land Hotel and out to far destinations on the battlefront. It was war, unexpected and threatening to a degree I had never known before, and while I never *personally* expected to be killed (which I learned later was a foolish fantasy), it was most certainly a war and people *were* dying on all fronts and the radio was blaring code words for call-ups and there were black-outs and long hours in bomb shelters and newscasts and more newscasts.

People poured into the country from everywhere: soldiers returning to fight, volunteers coming to cover jobs and pick produce for those who had been called up....everyone who could catch a plane. One of those who flew over was an old friend, Noam Saks (now known as Noam Zion), who left Minot, ND, where he had been serving as a Rabbi for the High Holidays. He arrived as soon as he could catch a flight. While I worked in the post office, he worked in a flour factory, and then, when the war wound down, he stayed, and we linked up and began to study Talmud together. He had made Aliya, deciding to stay with his People in their homeland, and leaving unfinished work on his PhD back in the States.

I went home again in August. My year was up. In January of 1975, still feeling the un-ease of the post-War aftermath, I went back to Israel, this time carrying $955.00 of my friends' money to give out to worthy individuals and projects. It was either on that trip or the next one during the summer or the summer after that that I ran into Noam again. This time he had met a certain Marcella, a young woman from Belgium, and though they were not yet engaged, it seemed likely they would marry. Somewhere in our re-union conversation, I told them I had this Tzedakah money to distribute, and somewhere shortly thereafter Marcella said I should meet this woman called Hadassah Levi who had a day-care center for re-tarded children.

I *did* meet her, and we gave her $100, a very large contribution in those days. Since then we've become very close friends.

That was the pattern: Summers in Israel, the rest of the year back in the States. Summers making rounds of the Tzedakah projects, re-meeting the people, getting updates on their work, sharing high moments. During one of my returns-to-America, Hadassah became seriously ill and spent an extended period of time in the hospital. While she was there she noticed a number of babies with Down's Syndrome that had been left behind. And some of them were being neglected, even to the point of being left near open windows in Wintertime.

I know people will object, insisting this doesn't happen and didn't happen, not in Israel, not in other places, but abandonment and neglect of babies with vary-ing disabilities are only a small portion of the many horror stories Hadassah has to tell. Anyone who reads about this may still object, but they should contact Hadas-sah to see her documented evidence. (I, myself, even heard a similar story this year of an American mother who, some 11 or 12 years before, had been offered "options" by the hospital staff when she gave birth to a baby with Down's Syndrome. She refused the "options", the child came home with the parents, and the daughter will become a bat mitzvah in the near future.)

The story becomes more and more amazing. This Hadassah Levi, deathly ill, made a solemn vow — if she recovered, she would take these babies and raise them. Which is exactly what happened.

HADASSAH'S KIDS

The youngest baby Hadassah ever took in was two hours old. The Gang (in Hebrew, "The Chevra") of kids who now range in age from 8 to 12, are intense and warm. Everyone who visits gets to know them right away because they come up to you, put out their arms, and demand hugs. Strong hugs, mighty hugs....for they are *very* strong children. (Another Horror Story: A government doctor came by on a regular inspection and asked Hadassah why she was wasting such good food on them. Why didn't she stay at the level of the government regulations? Some other official told her that the mortality rate was too low; she wasn't making room fast enough for new babies.)

They are strong because they are fed well, loved well, and have a Hadassah Levi to take care of them, despite a weight of odds-against-success few have to endure in their lifetimes. When you see the kids in a group, you might immediately think that some of them don't belong here because they certainly don't *look like* people with Down's Syndrome. People with Down's are *supposed* to look shorter and stockier and have rounder faces and a certain eye configuration and a tongue that often moves in and out of the mouth. Not so with most of Hadassah's Gang. She has developed a dietary regimen that has eliminated the "Down's Look" to a greater or lesser degree. Many specialists in the field have come to recognize her work in this area, theory-made-reality. Hadassah is no simple warm, loving mother figure (though she is that, too); she knows all there is to know about the scientific aspects of Down's Syndrome, and the psychology and physiology and sociology of the issue. Pick any sub-topic in the field, and she is an authority.

Furthermore, there are still many people who when asked to describe the nature of Down's Syndrome will suggest that the people with Down's die young, perhaps in their 20's or 30's. That is simply not true. People who have Down's Syndrome can, and ought to, live as long as anyone else — with the appropriate living situation and additional care that might go with some heart problems, muscle-tone problems, co-ordination problems, and slow-development problems. However, none of these complications is *necessarily* life-shortening if an appropriate life-environment is provided.

I love Hadassah for many reasons, but one of them is that she is an iconoclast, blasting away at the myths. But do not be mistaken: she is not raising these children as one might raise and test laboratory rats — just to prove some point or make some great scientific breakthrough. To the contrary, she is raising them because they are human beings who happen to have an extra chromosome and some additional special needs, and because she loves them intensely and beautifully and because no one else wanted them.

MA'ON LATINOK

Ma'on LaTinok, which simply means "A Home for Infants", is where these children spent their first years under Hadassah's care. Most of that time the Ma'on was located in a big house on a side street in Ramat Gan, set off the road about 100 feet. There the kids had rooms and a front yard to play in and other play areas and fine food and loving, faithful workers...and Hadassah. But then the troubles began with the neighbors.

The last couple of years that Hadassah was in the Ramat Gan house, she was in and out of court: neighbors wanted her out. It's an old story that sounds like "No Jews or dogs" signs, or, as Tip O'Neill recalls, signs about jobs that said "NINA", which was an abbreviation for "No Irish Need Apply". As I accumulate file drawers full of magazine and newspaper articles about issues like these, I see a new trend in America — the elderly. People in certain neighborhoods are campaigning in zoning boards to keep *them* out of the neighborhood.

With retarded people, things can get vicious — not the retarded people, but the neighbors. I have an article where, before the residents moved into a group home for retarded adults, some vigilante came by and blew out the front windows with a shotgun. Another, for a Jewish group home in the Detroit area, an arsonist did the trick, gutting the home. (It is to the credit of the Jewish Association of Retarded Citizens — who, along with the Jewish Foundation for Group Homes in Washington, stands in the forefront of this movement in the Jewish community — the Detroit group fixed up the house and opened it....despite the torching.)

When I ask teen-agers why they think people don't want group homes for retarded people in their neighborhoods, they give many ostensibly reasonable answers (though they don't believe these things themselves): (1) they're different, (2) people think they're dangerous, (3) people are afraid for their children's safety, (4) they're loud, (5) they're sloppy, and (6) property values. I am always amazed that a teen-ager should know anything about property values, but I inform them that studies show that — even if property values go down somewhat in the short term (which doesn't always happen) — they return to normal afterwards, and so, that, too, is a trumped-up excuse hiding an ugly bigotry that should scare all of us.

There are worse scenarios, too, abuses of all sorts. To name a few: a physician teaching her medical students how to do rectal examinations on retarded children in an institution, without any attempt at obtaining consent from family or guardians (the practice has since stopped, after a court case); an eminent physician, ultimately a Nobel Prize Winner, an equally-eminent medical school, and drug companies testing drugs and performing experiments on mentally ill individuals in institutions, without any informed consent (also stopped after a court case), and

Hadassah Levi (far right) with some of her "Gang."

Hadassah, relaxing in Jerusalem.

even reports in the summer of 1987 of drug experiments on elderly people in 16 nursing homes in Phoenix without their consent (some of the nursing-home operators received kickbacks from the drug companies). Underlying all these cases is a simple principle: the "guinea pigs" are vulnerable and defenseless, no one will find out, and, in the minds of the abusers, the victims are all somehow less-than-human.

This is where Hadassah Levi comes in, and people like her wherever they are. She is the ultimate Anti-Abuser. She is the person who screams and argues and fights small and large opponents to remind The Abusers that Human is Human. She has seen so much ugliness in her battles in court, and she saw more of the same insensitivity as she went from place to place seeking out a new home for the children. She heard and saw things no one should ever hear or see. And, while it is true that the kids were outgrowing the home in Ramat Gan, and it was becoming time to move, the transition to a new home should never have been so arduous.

Some of the neighbors stood against her. Some of the municipal bureaucracy stood against her. And some of the national bureaucracy fought her. I remember two visits with her as she paced the hallways and dining room of the Knesset (Israel's Parliament), as she buttonholed members of the legislature and sat in offices of members of Knesset, pleading her case, winning occasional victories and other times going down in momentary defeat. Still, in all, along the way she gained friends and good publicity from the courts and the media. Sides were taken, and, despite the exhaustion and disappointments, Hadassah found many, many new friends, journalists in particular, who heard her story and wrote about her. It is an incredibly touching — and very volatile — subject.

A solution has been reached — finally. When Hadassah's lease in Ramat Gan expired, and when she could not secure a new location, she temporarily put the children in a place in Jerusalem, a government institution. She thought they would stay there about a month....surely, she thought, she would find them a new home. But the month became two months and then six and then a year and finally a little more than a year. The institution was not a good place. The kids' health was getting worse; they were getting little of the unique attention and care that they had always received from Hadassah.

Then, a group known as Jerusalem Elwyn Institutes began negotiations to take over the institution. Elwyn has a series of sheltered workshops for mentally disabled individuals in Jerusalem, excellent projects, first-class by any standards. Elwyn originated in Philadelphia decades ago, with an equally fine reputation there. They have expertise; they have a network of caring administrators and workers and fund raisers and support staff. They know Human is Human. By the time this book appears, the takeover will be complete, Hadassah will be back in full swing with her children and other children in Elwyn's radius of activity, and there is hope that a number of new babies (who are waiting for someone like Hadassah) will come into Elwyn, and she will begin a new cycle. Hadassah, now in her 50's, has been worn down by The Good Fight, but we all have reason to believe she will summon up a second glorious burst of energy.

When things stabilize, there will be more talk of foster homes and adoptive homes and more extensive educational opportunities and a whole world of new possibilities, including a Great Integration into the flow of society. That is good news, not only for Hadassah's Gang, but also for society itself. For now, we will have to wait, watch, and take it all in in the next few years to see how Hadassah's struggles and dreams are rewarded.

SOME ADDITIONAL GOOD STORIES

Adults who have met Hadassah and her Gang love her. For Rabbis Moshe Edelman and Ron Hoffberg, a standard slot on their synagogue tours' itinerary is a visit to the Ma'on. The Rabbis and their congregants are always deeply moved, as is to be expected. And there is a group in Connecticut, Chavurah Tzedakah, that has become attached to Hadassah's Kids. The group issues newsletters and has designed a poster and gives financial support and very-much-needed moral support. The kids are an important part of all these people's lives, though they are thousands of miles away.

But the best Hadassah stories are about kids, American and Canadian Jewish kids. For many summers, the teen-agers on the United Synagogue Youth Israel Pilgrimage would go to Ma'on LaTinok to meet Hadassah and her Gang. Now, teen-agers can be very teen-agey, but not here. I count it among the greatest joys of my life to watch these teen-agers from all over the United States and Canada fan out among Hadassah's kids (first when they were babies, now as growing children) and begin to play with them. Until that part of their summer adventure in Israel, some of the teen-agers seemed to project an image of shallow, silly people. That is, until they went to the Ma'on. There, the pseudo-cool-jocks and the ones with earrings (i.e., one earring for the boys) and the girls who concentrated *very* hard on painting their nails, there — with Hadassah and her kids — they showed their true colors....They were no longer locked into the myth of teen-agerhood. They could be their true selves, fully human, warm, intense, giving of themselves as they had never given before, and receiving an absolutely unique kind of giving and love in return.

Now, when they sit in clusters over coffee or soda, Jewish educators often lament the hardships of bringing content and depth to their students. They bewail the Sorrows-of-Plenty, the having-too-much which often plagues the kids and their decent chances at developing the better sensitivities. These educators ought to board a plane with their students and head for Hadassah and her Gang.

They will see Hadassah's kids stretch out their arms for a hug; and they will see hugs given in return...warm, natural hugs.

They will see Hadassah's kids stretch out their arms for a hug and a clear indication that they would like to be picked up and hugged better. No matter that they are no longer babies weighing 8 or 10 or 19 pounds, but hefty 9-and-10-and-11-year-olds. No matter that they grab your sunglasses and hat before you know what is happening or that they fiddle with your camera and snap a picture before you can catch them.

The educators will see frizbees and basketballs and toys flying all over the place, and most of all, people playing with people.

They will hear one Ostensibly Stereotypical Suburban Teen-ager, shedding his Ostensible Stereotypical Suburban Teen-agerhood, saying, "There I was playing with one baby, and there was this other one in the corner sitting all by herself, so I picked that one up, too." Imagine, two babies at once, all enjoying themselves (*all* meaning the babies and the teen-ager) as naturally as natural can possibly be.

The educators will watch the faces of the USY Pilgrims as Hadassah speaks to them of horrors and hope, secrecy and night-long vigils. They will see the teen-agers' faces alternate between a dumbstruck look and exhilaration.

They will read Hadassah's in albums where the USY'ers get to write down their thoughts at the end of the visit, words that are so moving, the reader weeps. Words of younger brothers and sisters whose older brothers and sisters had been there a year or two or three before and heard Hadassah and played with the kids and hugged and had their cameras snatched in play and mischievous smiles all around and who wrote their own words then in the album and went back and told their younger brothers and sisters what a great day they will have with Hadassah and her Gang when they get to Israel.

In sum, the educators will witness more magic and tears and smiles per-square-person than is considered average by the most distinguished psycho-statisticians.

When the USY'ers go home, they are somehow different. Besides all the wonders of Israel they have seen: the Sabbath in Jerusalem, the O-so-many kinds of Jewish people in-gathered from throughout the world, the Hebrew alive-as-alive-can-possibly-be, the rebuilding of the wasteland, the climb up Massada before dawn ....besides all those things that will change them, the day with Hadassah will change them.

The teen-agers will give speeches in their synagogues and youth groups and schools about this miracle-of-a-woman and her children.

They will show their pictures of the kids and tell their friends and family the names — for Hadassah and her Gang will no longer be just a bunch of faraway kids in some pamphlet they read about. They are real people, real children with hopes and dreams and justifiable expectations of what life has to offer.

Some of them will write their college entrance essays about Hadassah and her kids.

They will cringe when they hear the word "*ret*ard" (accent on the first syllable) — when they hear a child use it as a weapon and an insult — and they will be sorry they themselves had used the word, as so many of us did, thinking it was smart or cute.

They will raise money for Hadassah and her Gang and gather clothing for them and write letters to this most awesome woman.

And they will yearn to go back again to be a part of their lives.

For myself, this will be my 13th consecutive summer programming Tzedakah projects for the USY Pilgrims. People sometimes ask if I am tired of doing it, if it has become routine. After what I have described, I think they will know that I am just getting cranked up. We missed the summer of 1987 at Hadassah's place. They were in the government institution, and we couldn't make the arrangements. It is now May 10, 1988. In two months we begin again, and my life is now all waiting; I am waiting for the wonders upon wonders to happen again.

HADASSAH'S SOLDIER

Hadassah tells the following story with great emotion:

Not too long ago, Hadassah got a phone call from some young Israeli man saying, "I think you know where my sister is."

This young man, a soldier, remembered that, a few years before, his pregnant mother had gone into the hospital but when she came home, no baby came with her. The family story was unclear, but the soldier sensed that he did, indeed, have a baby sister, who would be six or seven by the time he found Hadassah.

He searched and asked and did out-of-the-ordinary detective work for over a year before he concluded his sister was one of those left behind in the hospital and was now under Hadassah's care. Hadassah knew he was right, but was wary nonetheless. It was the mother's secret, and Hadassah would only let him come if he promised not to tell the family.

He agreed.

When the soldier came to the Ma'on, a bunch of the kids were getting off a bus from school. He asked Hadassah not to tell him which one was his sister — he would pick her out himself. And so he did, weeping, Hadassah weeping, the staff weeping. It was a grand moment for all of them, and in no time at all, brother and sister felt very much like brother and sister.

At the time, the soldier was involved with a young woman. It looked like they would marry, and he explained to the woman that this person, his sister, was to be a part of their lives, an important part.

She agreed: they got married, and now they are regular visitors, being brother and sister-in-law as is expected, and also sharing some of their human goodheartedness with the other members of Hadassah's Gang.

My own personal quest continued, and I told Hadassah I wanted to meet this brother and his wife. She gave me a phone number, and I became a most welcome guest in their house more than once. Whenever I wanted to feel moments of exhilaration in my soul, I would go over there and have coffee with them and listen to them and talk to them. But mostly I would just sit and listen. They're young; his business is beginning to take hold; they have simple tastes and a simple lifestyle, and though this phrase will come up again and again, they are very real. As I said before, time is on hold for me — I cannot wait to get back to Jerusalem to see Hadassah and the kids, these two Real People, the young soldier and his wife.

And I think it is nice to end this tale of Hadassah and her Gang with an uplifting story, because, for all the frustration and anger and bureaucratic sabotage and ugliness, this is a story of hope, of human goodness and glory.

Hadassah Levi, POB 413, Givata'im, Israel. Phone: 09-929-265.

REFLECTIONS II

My teacher and friend, Rabbi Jack Riemer, recently gave me an article summarizing a survey sponsored by World Almanac. They asked five thousand highschool students who their heroes were. These are the results, in order of importance:

1. *Bill Cosby*
2. *Sylvester Stallone*
3. *Eddie Murphy*
4. *President Reagan*
5. *Chuck Norris*
6. *Clint Eastwood*
7. *Molly Ringwald*
8. *Rob Lowe*
9. *Arnold Schwartzeneggar*
10. *Don Johnson*

Now go back and read "Reflections: I".

MYRIAM MENDILOW

She was the first of my Mitzvah heroes. Our connection stretches back some 15 years to the time when my Mother told me that I had to go see Myriam Mendilow and her marvellous work with elderly people in Jerusalem, Life Line for the Old, (Yad LaKashish). Mom was insistent. I went, and became a convert to Mrs. Mendilow's vision of what it can be like to be old.

First, the background. Twenty-five years ago, Mrs. Mendilow was a most highly respected teacher in Israel's schools. Nowadays when you see her talking to kids about Life Line, you understand that she must have been The Teacher Everyone Always Wanted to Have. She hugs the kids, kisses them, hugs them again, looks intensely into their eyes and coaxes answers from them, Big Answers, like the answer to "Why do you think so many old people are miserable?" She is *very* intense. (Everyone should have at least one intense teacher sometime during their years of formal education.)

As a first-rate teacher she listened to her students and she paid careful attention to their laments of, "Why does my grandmother just sit around?" "Grandpa is such a nuisance." She heard more and more of this, and understood that the children were getting a warped perception of what it is to be old. For Mendilow, then in her early 50's, it was a tragic misunderstanding, and she set out to change the lives of both the elderly and the young alike. After all, "Zaken" in Hebrew means "An Elder", carrying connotations of respect. It means someone who has lived many years and has acquired a unique wisdom, a certain feeling for life that is worthy to be taught to others.

There was a period of time when she set up clubs for elderly people — places where a number of activities took place. Then she made her breakthrough: she went to the Ministry of Labor and asked for a teacher, someone to teach bookbinding to elderly people. She would have old people repair the damaged books of Jerusalem's schoolchildren. The children would then come to see the bookbinders, admire not only their work but the elderly bookbinders themselves, a magic moment of insight would flash in the young people's minds, and a great wrong would be righted. She got her teacher, and then began to pull beggars off of the streets, as well as old people who were sitting in rooms waiting for death....and she put them to work.

It was at this stage of her activities that she became known as "HaMeshuga'at", "The Crazy Woman".

Now there are many people who think the Jerusalem beggars add a certain touch of romance to the Holy City. Mendilow thought it was an outrage, and she prodded the beggars and berated them for having no self-image; she shouted at them and pushed them until they came to her workshop in the slum area called Musrara on the old border with Jordan. Musrara was right next to what used to be called No Man's Land, and you could see Jordanian soldiers, rifles in hand, in the not-too-great distance. She specifically wanted it there because that is where many of them lived, and, I suppose, without much money to start this Life Line for the Old, she could keep the expenses to a minimum.

And this is where a lot of people who consider Mitzvah work from a theoretical standpoint often go astray. When I ask teen-agers how they think Life Line got started, many of them think the first step was getting substantial sums of money. Mrs. Mendilow will tell you she started with nothing, plunged in, and worried about details like money later on as Life Line expanded. Seeing how the place has grown to more than a dozen workshops and several related projects, her point is well taken and worth considering when we, ourselves, make plans to launch our own projects. A sense of vision, Mitzvah-creativity, and persistence *always* take precedence over funding.

Thus, starting with nothing (except the bookbinding teacher and a handful of soon-to-be-former-beggars and other elderly people who mistakenly thought they were going to die soon), she managed to get a room for the workshop. It was really a hovel or a shack that had been used by one of Jerusalem's burial societies to prepare the bodies for a funeral. What did it matter? As long as there was a place to get old people working at the bookbindery. Nowadays The Elders re-bind all of the books of Jerusalem's schoolchildren. Life Line is awarded the contract not because the municipality feels sorry for a bunch of "old folks", but, quite to the contrary, it is because Life Line puts in the best bid for the contract and because The Elders do the best job. Indeed, after an hour or a morning or a hundred mornings at Life Line mingling with the workers, you will discover that there is no reason to feel sorry for anyone anywhere within its precincts.

When I take teen-agers and older friends through Life Line, this is the way I do a tour: an introductory discussion with me, a little fire from Mrs. Mendilow, and then a walking tour — the bookbindery, then to ceramics (unique jewelry, pottery, tile painting, some leatherwork combined with ceramic pieces, Mezuzot, Menorot, other ritual objects), to the carton-making workshop (boxes for commercial businesses), upstairs to the metal shop, a little more upstairs to two workshops where they are doing needlework (embroidery, crocheting, knitting, toys, sweaters, tablecloths, too many things to mention; one is a "finishing" workshop, the bulk of the work being done at home by various people, then finished at Life Line), up to the patio and bakery (baked goods of all kinds served as a snack to The Elders), weaving workshop (now making Talitot, among other things), triple workshop with all kinds of needlecrafts, down a bunch of stairs, brief stop in the place where the giant looms are, down again through the central courtyard, out the front gate, a left, past the second-hand clothing store, into the main kitchen where the Meals-on-Wheels are prepared (for 200 people), the Mo'adon (the meeting hall where the choir practices, where afternoon activities take place, where meetings and parties are held), a stop at the shoemaker (who repairs their shoes), into the carpentry shop (where they repair all manner of things), out and down the hill to the workshop for people with disabilities (all kinds of needlework), back up the street, to the right, walk 100 feet, a right, back through the main gate, into the store ("The Elder Craftsman", where you may feast your eyes on, and purchase, an astonishing variety of items that are made at Life Line). By the end of the morning, you will have seen a good couple of hundred people at work there, and there are approximately 450 people that Mrs. Mendilow reaches with all the Life Line projects combined. And they are *happy* people.

That is the tour. You will need a good, solid morning to go through it all, and it is best to come around 8:15. You will see The Elders arriving by foot, by bus, by car, by special van for those who are in wheelchairs, Elders with one cane, with two canes, with all kinds of illnesses and disabilities and weaknesses put into the back of their minds as they go to work. (I remember one man with a cane crossing the street to get to Life Line. A big Egged bus bore down on him. Forgetting the cane, he ran across the street.)

(As you walk around, *take note*: there are stairs everywhere. These steps are good for many of The Elders. People whom you would think could never make it up and down the steps go up and down these steps. After all, they *do* have to get to work, and work is upstairs for many of them. So they *do* have to get up the stairs. No one gets babied at Life Line. Babies should be babied, not old people.)

This is the essence of the place: it is where the old people come to work. No one lives there. It's not an old-age home nor any kind of institution. There is no presence of people in white medical coats (I forgot to mention the volunteer dentists in the dentist's office whom you can meet on the tour; they wear white coats. So I lied a little.)

There is no odor of medicine (or, for that matter, worse smells visitors to some institutions for the elderly have come to associate with a few such institutions), and no one hovers over The Elders to see if they are taking this pill or that capsule or some other remedy. Most people end up taking less medication than they used to — after they have settled into the Life Line routine. (Again I lied a little. There are a couple of volunteer doctors who have an office off the courtyard. They can see people there and attend to some of their medical problems. But they are *not* in the courtyard or workshops. They are *not* hovering like a grey eminence throughout Life Line.)

As you walk around the workshops, you will see people who were born in Algeria, Morocco, Tunisia, Libya, Iraq, Iran, Egypt, Ethiopia, Israel (of course), Rumania, Hungary, Russia, Poland, Bulgaria, Greece, Italy, The Netherlands, France, England, Germany, Austria, Argentina, South Africa, the United States, and probably some other countries I have overlooked.

There are survivors of the Holocaust, and people who remember Pogroms and the Russian Revolution, and riots in Arab lands, and secret border-crossings and bribing guards to be free, and long journeys by boat, by plane, by donkey or by horse or by foot.

They are all there.

I have always said that, if you wanted to learn Modern Jewish History, this is the place to come to in order to get the facts.

Jews and non-Jews work there: Arabs, Christians, and Jews side-by-side, a little pocket of peace in the Holy City.

You will also become aware of the fact that The Elders get a paycheck. The salary is more like pocket money — Mrs. Mendilow hardly has the funding to pay substantial wages — but Israel's National Insurance and other programs provide a safety net that more or less guarantees that no one will sink to the lowest levels of poverty. Each person is paid the same amount, whether they are producing pieces of clay for a necklace or knitting or crocheting the fanciest dresses.

I particularly love the store, The Elder Craftsman. So much of what is being made in the workshops is gathered in one shop. I always tell my friends they should never purchase anything there because they feel sorry for old people; they should only buy the item if they think it is beautiful and they want to own it or give it to someone as a gift. The products win awards again and again in fairs and exhibitions within Israel and outside the country, and they are now being sold in the United States. [Call Diane Lilly, 301-299-4521, in Potomac, MD.] A while back, 50% of Life Line's budget came from sales in the store, though I don't know today's percentages.

At the end of the morning, after the talks, the tour, the time in the store, people generally feel a sense of amazement. They are dazzled, and say to themselves, "How could so many daily miracles happen in one place?" Mrs. Mendilow has been screaming for years about how simple it is, and now I, her student, will add some more rantings and ravings on her behalf: it *is* simple....You take some old people who are bored, who feel senseless, left out, depressed and useless, and you put them to work making gorgeous things. That seems simple enough. Keeping things simple has proven that the Elders will feel better, be happier, live longer, and inspire young people and give the young people the feeling of looking forward to being old. Simple enough.

A basic rule we could derive from Mrs. Mendilow and Life Line would then seem to be: don't over-complicate.

I ask myself — now that Life Line is 25 years old — if you were to take the grand total of years Mrs. Mendilow has added to the lives of the people who have worked there, how many thousands of years would it be? Furthermore, since the much-battered term "quality of life" is bandied about in the medical profession and various disciplines of social service, perhaps the medical professionals and social service professionals should make a pilgrimage to Life Line. When they see a considerable number of older people who were ostensibly half-dead "come back to life", it might just be time for all of us to reconsider our understanding of the Nature of Things — old age and aging, what exactly "quality of life" might be, why this place is so suffused with human happiness and contentment. The sum-total of years — good, happy years — that Mendilow has added to the lives of The Elders must be truly staggering.

Mrs. Mendilow is a fanatic. She has turned me into a fanatic, and so I will take a little space and continue to be a little fanatical.

I have visited a number of old-age residences in the United States and Canada, both old-age homes and independent living situations for the elderly. Many of them have fine workshops and are producing gorgeous products which they sell in their stores. But Myriam Mendilow's contention is that a Life Line for the Old will *prevent* — and most certainly delay — some people's need to enter such housing arrangements, particularly old-age homes. It is safe to say she hates old-age homes, though she recognizes the need for them in extreme situations. It is equally safe to say that she is depressed by what she has seen when she, herself, has visited old-age homes. There is no question in her mind that there are many people in old-age homes who do not have to live there. If society would provide The Elders with Life-Line-like opportunities for independence, skills, and vigorous, creative work, they would not decline as they have been declining in society as we know it in America. ("Decline" means *psychologically* and *emotionally*, as well as physically. All three are inextricably tied to each other.)

As I have said, Mrs. Mendilow is a fanatic. Someone from the United States once came and asked her why his workshops for the elderly weren't working out. His place had invested thousands of dollars in fine equipment. She asked him, "Where are the workshops located?" He answered that they were right there in the building. She said, "Dismantle everything and move the equipment two blocks away." He did, and the workshops worked. The old people had to get up, get out of bed, dress, put on a coat, brave heat or cold, snow or rain, get on a van or bus, and go to a workplace that was somewhere other than the place that was their home. It worked, and it was simple. (I think he bought her a new electric typewriter as a thank-you.)

Mendilow is full of initiative, always expanding Life Line's scope, planning new projects, building on the basic vision. In the past few years she has brought young people to work at Life Line, young people with physical and/or mental disabilities, to work side-by-side with The Elders. And it works. There are people who come from mental institutions during the day; they come to work, and many get better, if not always totally "well". There are adjustments and tensions; that is true. But call it "work therapy" or whatever you want....the idea is still the same idea, and it still works.

There are crises at Life Line. There is no question that there are crises. In a place where so many people come with so many years of psychological and emotional baggage and physical limitations, there has got to be a number of crises small and large. But the place not only functions well, it thrives.

When it comes to fighting for the rights of the Elders with the "outside world", Mrs. Mendilow can be very tough. She has to be, because the stakes are very high: the lives and dignity of The Elders are very precious things. The Mayor of Jerusalem is her friend, and I am sure she has backed him into a corner more than once, insisting on appropriate benefits for her people. So, too, other government officials up and down the ladder of authority....I would imagine many have cringed when they knew she was coming to demand their rights. And that is good.

Myriam Mendilow and one of the elders of Life Line for the Old.

Thousands of elderly Jerusalemites would not have reached such happy old age over the past 25 years if she weren't as high-powered as she is.

It is hard to believe that Mrs. Mendilow is in her late 70's. Her intensity and strength persist.

Usually I feel comfortable with Mrs. Mendilow's evangelism-on-behalf-of-the-Elders that has rubbed off on me. On occasion I overstep my bounds because of my enthusiasm for her and for Life Line, and I say things that some people resent. But still, in all, I prefer the fire and the drive she has instilled in me. Most of all, Mrs. Mendilow has so changed my grasp of old age, I cannot re-orient myself enough to remember what I used to think and feel before I first came into the courtyard at Life Line. For that I — and thousands of others like me — are grateful.

THE USY KIDS

I have been going back to Mrs. Mendilow and Life Line every summer for the past twelve years now. As the Tzedakah Resource Person for the United Synagogue Youth Israel Pilgrimage, I get to take anywhere from 500 to 650 teen-agers from across North America to meet Mrs. Mendilow and to tour Life Line. And I will do it again this summer, because it is only then that I feel alive-to-the-utmost.

There is electricity in the air when the teen-agers arrive. I know what is going to happen to them (though there is always some variation): they are about to meet someone unique. Mrs. Mendilow is not only unlike anyone they have ever met before, she is most likely someone they had never thought existed or could exist. They will soar very high with the exhilaration of Life Line, and they will be moved. Many of them will be charged up to go back and change things in their home towns. For some, it will be a wrenching experience, as they recall elderly members of their own families who might have benefited from such a place....and there was no such place locally to be found. Some will even become smaller-scale fanatics, spreading the word with Mendilow-like enthusiasm. For most, it will be a morning of pure joy.

I love to watch Mrs. Mendilow "working the crowd", making her appearance, looking like "just one of the old people". Everything changes once she begins to talk and the teen-agers realize they are coming face to face with a visionary, a person who will not tolerate injustice and senseless human debasement, a powerful human force that makes things happen. They cannot believe how old she is. They cannot believe her first workers were beggars. They cannot believe it started in a hole in the wall where people used to wash bodies in preparation for burial. She awes them. (I love it.)

Mrs. Mendilow does not talk down to them. And she doesn't play games. She makes demands; she wants them to change their attitudes and actions towards the elderly *right now*. She desperately wants them to join her in her work, to spread the message, the ever-so-simple message. It is not enough that there is one Life Line — there have to be many, she insists...Everywhere. She talks to them, listens to them, asks questions and gets answers, and reacts to the answers. She urges and pushes and sometimes shouts emphatically when they are aligned just right with her visions, or shouts just emphatically when they have clung to their out-dated myths about old age. With the kids, she is in all her glory. She is truly awesome. (I love it.)

There are other teen-age groups that come, too, nowadays. NFTY groups from the Reform Movement, community groups from Houston, Denver, other places. And adult groups come through, too. American Jewish Congress tours always stop there; synagogue tours stop there; some Jewish Federation groups stop there, and others. But it is with the kids that Mrs. Mendilow radiates so wonderfully and lays out her glorious dreams so expansively. She wants to make dreamers and visionaries out of all of the kids. Even more, she wants all the people who hear her to act on those dreams and visions and pull and push and tug and scream until the dreams and visions are real, as real as Life Line for the Old.

Mrs. Mendilow has many awards, many laurels. By the time she is through with the kids, they know that no one ever should rest on his or her laurels. There is too much good Mitzvah work left to be done. With twenty-five years of Life Line behind her, and a magnificent Palace of Dignity at the disposal of Jerusalem's Elders, it always seems like she is just getting started. She is forever revving up for a new challenge. That is very good for the kids to hear — not from me — but from Mrs. Mendilow herself.

By the time the morning is over, I am drained. So many things have been happening, so many levels of interaction between Mrs. Mendilow and the kids, between the kids and The Elders, between myself and the kids and elders and Mrs. Mendilow. Back in the United States and Canada I will run into the kids again here and there. If we consider the fact that the first groups to go through Life Line began in 1976, there are already hundreds of no-longer-kids out there who are pushing 30 and moving quickly into positions of power in the Jewish community if they so choose. How good it feels, reviewing the last 12 years of my work with the kids and Mrs. Mendilow....that there are 6,000 USY'ers (at least), and a few thousand other teen-agers and former teen-agers out there who have had those moments at Life Line with this incredible woman. They know that power is just a tool for Mitzvahs.

Maybe they will someday earn the honorific of "The Crazy One", bearing the title with pride, knowing they were trained by "HaMeshuga'at" - "The Crazy Woman of Jerusalem", who really isn't so crazy after all.

Life Line for the Old, 14 Shivtei Yisrael St., Jerusalem, 287-831.

REFLECTIONS III

I so much wanted to do a story that would begin with, "And then the baby died...." or "The child was as good as dead."

I wanted a shocking opening and the whole book to be sizzling, inventive, maybe even a mystery, with bullets and silencers and trenchcoats and coded messages, and a dozen exotic cities as settings, the kind of book you would read on the plane or train; the kind that sells millions of copies instead of just my usual four or five thousand. The kind of book that gives a printing history where the second printing of 100,000 copies is listed as a month after the original publication date.

It would have been my first novel after many other books of poetry and prose and study texts and humor and everything else.

But the material wouldn't take shape that way at all. So this book had to turn out to be a different kind of story. For some reason I just couldn't write the other kind of book. Maybe next time.

These people, these normal people, these Mitzvah heroes take hold of you and sit inside of your mind and shake your metabolism and won't let go.

All those stories I read (and made fun of) about writers writing books to spill something out of their guts — this time it is true for me. I need to get it down on paper, but not in order to move on to other things. I don't want to move on (move on to where?) I just want to get a better hold of these people, see them just a little more clearly, formulate new questions about them.

It's like, having taken Elementary Physics and enjoying it, you wanted to move on to Advanced Physics. Having enjoyed my first and second and third and twentieth encounters with the Heroes, I feel it is time for me to get from Elementary Mitzvah Heroes 101 to Advanced Mitzvah Heroes 201.

When I get into my particularly sentimental or mushy moods, I think I would have them carve my epitaph with the following words, "His life was very full. He strolled and talked with angels."

CELESTE McKINLEY, JOSEPH LORDI, AND ALICE MOSINIAK

Poverty, hunger, and homelessness are so tied together that anyone involved in one area usually ends up working in all three. The increase in numbers of poor, hungry, and homeless people in the past decade has devastated the consciousness of many Americans. There is a need for a broad re-thinking, *very* broad, to re-discover our principles of creating a society based on Tzedek — Justice and Equity, so that everyone might have a decent and fair chance to make a living and have a full and long life with sufficient food, clothing, shelter, and warmth.

There are many experts on the subject, and many of them have important truths to tell. One such expert recently told the members of the Allocations Committee of MAZON-A Jewish Response to Hunger, that in 1983, more than 50% of the households making $7,000 or less paid out more than 60% of their income for rent. So some of the problem is critically tied to low-income housing....No question about it, and it is expected to get much worse.

Another expert, Dr. J. Larry Brown, Chairman of the Physician Task Force on Hunger in America, offers a multitude of statistics and hard facts, insights and first-hand stories in his book *Living Hungry in America*. Arms-and-Butter is just one such issue. One of Brown's friends calculated that, if the United States government had theoretically spent $1,000,000 *a day* since 1990 years ago, we would not have spent half the money the Reagan Administration has spent on arms. That's

$1,588 trillion (defense outlays, 1981-1987)
$726,847 billion (1990 years X 365.25 days X $1 million)
$726,847 billion X 2 = $1,453 trillion.

In another passage, Brown offers another comparison: "One B-1 Bomber...costs approximately four hundred million dollars....That amount of money would provide school lunches for a quarter-million hungry people for a decade. Two CVN nuclear attack carriers cost over seven billion dollars. That amount, used to strengthen existing nutrition programs, would virtually eradicate hunger in America."

Brown criss-crossed the country with physicians and professors for two years, going into homes, talking to local citizens and local and national government officials. This was no mere statistical print-out kind of study with computers and professors number-crunching in an office at the Harvard School of Public Health. Brown's was a human, a *very* human look at hungry people in this country.

There are so many shattering stories: empty refrigerators for elderly people in Vermont and New Hampshire; frightening numbers of low-birth-weight babies being born among the poor — attributable to a great extent to insufficient nutrition for poor and hungry pregnant mothers, children who are sad when summer comes because there won't be a lunch that day, to mention but a few. In short, the American safety net has been seriously weakened. (I took particular note of this when I was at a Jewish education conference in London. The stories did not ring true to my British counterparts.)

Brown is right, as are so many other activists and lobbyists in this field. Congress, local legislatures, all kinds of public officials must be pushed to act. More new heroes, advocates of the poor, hungry, and homeless, Tzaddikim in the sense of those who do Tzedek, Who Bring Justice, must appear and make things happen on the grand scale. They will be people who will free up a billion dollars and more and legislate better benefit programs and provide for the most basic, humanly decent needs for the people because they are entitled to the benefits. Those are the kinds of things we thought of and dreamed of as schoolchildren when we first learned about The Founding of America. They were Ideals-Turned-Real. That is why we are horrified when we read stories and articles about homeless people being set on fire by "mischievous" kids or adults who find them in some way offensive to their sensibilities. Legislation and the very fiber of our national, state, and local programs have to change.

And yet, there is The Great Meantime.

Even while we take upon ourselves this massive campaign, people have to be fed, sheltered and clothed. All our lobbying and pressuring and campaigning still would not free us from feeding, clothing, and housing people who need these basic things *now*. Indeed, legislators and lobbyists should also be simultaneously feeding, housing, and clothing people on a most personal basis. Second-level Mitzvah work (meetings, conferences, colloquia, smoke-filled rooms) is only one side of the commitment.

In the general community, food banks, shelters, and soup kitchens have sprung up everywhere. A multitude of people respond daily, cooking and scrubbing pots, washing sheets and laying out beds.

Daddy Bruce Randolph in Denver has done his Thanksgiving and Christmas meals for thousands of hungry people for years, right out of his modest Daddy Bruce's Barbecue. (Twice I've tried to meet him, this man in his late 80's, the last time getting as close as his restaurant, but it was closed. I'll try again, soon.)

Kroger's puts out an ad for its grocery store and says, "We at Kroger are concerned about Hunger in America and we have committed to do our part in solving this national problem. At Kroger, edible food will not be thrown away. Agencies who feed the needy have been assigned in every Kroger location we serve, and will be picking up merchandise regularly from our stores. We urge all retailers of the food industry to share our concern and join in the effort to DONATE — DON'T DUMP!"

Bruce Springsteen, The Boss, donated $10,000 and $25,000 per concert on a recent tour for local food banks and for unemployed workers who were down on their luck....nearly $500,000.

Kenny Rogers asked people to bring a can of food to his concerts (as other entertainers did and still do): 2,000,000 pounds of food in 71 concerts.

And there are benefit concerts everywhere.

And in the Jewish community things are happening.

Kosher food banks in New York, Dallas (through Jewish Family Service, feeding 10,000 people in one year, Jews and non-Jews), Los Angeles (Sova), Chicago (The Ark), Philadelphia, Boston (started by a small synagogue, Shaare Tefila in Norwood), to name a few.

And Kosher meals-on-wheels and meals-on-heels (delivered on foot by volunteers) and Cook-for-a-Friend programs, and Kosher soup kitchens, like the one Rabbi Jory Lang started in the Miami area.

And a Jewish Community Center staff member in one city who went to grocery stores and Sunday brunches at local restaurants and asked for the leftovers; who prepared a fine meal, and then went with a friend to feed the hungry of her city. The two of them reached 40 people the first time out. And they continue to do so. It's now called "Kavod Caterers" ("Dignity Caterers"), and they are feeding 100 people every week.

And a young woman in Chicago who connected hunger and homelessness to her bat mitzvah celebration in a very real fashion....She invited her extended family and friends, and the other guests to join the immediate family on Sunday for a post bat mitzvah gathering: Everyone was invited to bring bag lunches and meet at a specific street corner. Once there, they would personally distribute the food to hungry and homeless people.

And Jewish students at the University of Pennsylvania and other campuses doing their weekly labors-of-love at the local soup kitchens.

And MAZON-A Jewish Response to Hunger asking people to contribute 3% of the cost of a catered event or convention, the money going to feed hungry people. Now nearly four years old, MAZON has almost reached $1,000,000 a year. Every six months the number of grant applications grows at a startling rate.

And something as simple as overcoats for the cold Winter nights on the street: Marian Slotin, a woman in Charleston, SC, who personally gathered 200 of them and got them to people who needed them (besides holding her birthday party in the local shelter).

And Ranan Engelhart, whose idea is catching on — having people bring extra overcoats to his bar mitzvah party. Eighty coats came in that one night, and the following year, when his synagogue planned a coat drive, he (The Greatest Living Expert on Coat Drives in the Synagogue) was appointed chairman, with 100 more coats taken in.

And a post-script to Ranan Engelhart's story: Richard Gelfond of Great Neck, NY, cleaned 14,000 overcoats free of charge at his Clean Streets USA dry cleaning chain. They were overcoats the Salvation Army had gathered for the children of New York who needed them. Gelfond says he was ready to do 100,000 coats if necessary. (When I daydream, I picture a Ranan Engelhart growing up to be a Richard Gelfond, moving up to bigger and bigger projects.)

The list could go on for pages and pages. There are some relatively small-time projects and some truly immense projects. None of them is just a "band-aid" for the sore and aching body. To the contrary, they are real-live acts of goodness done by people and companies who know someone will be less hungry or less cold because of their efforts. It is, as Jewish tradition calls it, Tikkun Olam-Fixing Up the World.

Each project bespeaks someone's individual heroism. These are heroic acts in that it takes courage to step out of the Apathetic Crowd to do what has to be done, to get down into the mud, and sometimes the blood, guts and even gore of Mitzvah work. It may not be the same kind of courage as that of the man who jumped into the freezing Potomac River to save victims of the Air Florida plane crash, but it is still courage. It is just courage of a different type, and it is equally admirable. Indeed, more people are capable of the latter kind of courage than the former. I just don't know what I would do in an emergency situation that would involve risking life and limb. But the other kind of courage is more beckoning, more open to everyone.

This past year I have met three heroic individuals, all of them involved in food bank operations.

I need to tell their stories.

CELESTE McKINLEY

It was the Big Time at last. I had arrived: I finally got an invitation to play Vegas. The Jewish Community had invited me out there to give a speech on Tzedakah. It wasn't exactly a headline act at the clubs...but still it was Las Vegas.

It was also a chance to meet one of the Mitzvah heroes I had read about.

I arrived around 11:30 Saturday night and wandered in and out of casinos till about 4:00 a.m., playing a little blackjack and electronic poker, watching the people gamble away big and small sums. It was glittery and fun. Early the next morning, Dr. Harry Goldberg called. He had made the arrangements for my trip and had succeeded in tracking down the phone number of one Celeste McKinley, the woman in one of my newspaper articles.

It was a miserable day, rainy and chilly, but an old camper pulled up in front of the hotel and I was invited in to ride to Gleaners, Celeste's food bank. I must tell the truth: the camper was a little seedy, and besides Celeste and her husband, David, there were two dogs inside romping around. I was afraid I was going to wind up in the middle of some bizarre surrealistic story far from home on a rainy and chilly day in Las Vegas. All the elements were there.

David drove us to this *huge* warehouse and Celeste told her story:

One day, about six years ago, November 1, 1981, to be exact, Celeste said to David, "I'll go down to the grocery store and see if there is some leftover produce they'll give us for Precious." Precious is their pet cockatoo who lives at Gleaners and has the run of the office. A nice friendly bird, white, with the appropriate cockatoo head crest. Since we had a pet parrot when I grew up, I knew that birds like these not only ate seeds, but also liked carrots, bananas and other fruits and vegetables.

So Celeste went to the store and the manager said that, for sure, there was produce she could take home, and, for sure, she should come back the next day for more. It soon became clear to Celeste that this grocery store, and other stores like it, were throwing out enormous amounts of food, food perfectly fit for people to eat. So she made arrangements to make regular pick-ups and started feeding people.

Now Gleaners handles 400,000 pounds of food a month, feeding 700 people a day, 20,000 people a month — *free*. (I called yesterday. Celeste had just gotten a truckload of cabbage recently — 35,000 pounds of it, and now it is almost gone.) (A recent article in the *Indianapolis Star* reported that groups of people who glean the fields in Northeast Indiana harvest enough food to feed 45,000 people every month. The food bank director over there estimates that the United States wastes about 60,000,000 *tons* of grain, fruits and vegetables a year, which would be enough to feed 49 million people a day.) There is no limit on bread and produce and many other items. People come in and take as much as they need. There are limits on meat and some other items, but mostly it's a simple story: people simply come into Gleaners and get what they need.

The people have to have some sort of identification that indicates that they do, indeed, need the food, but Celeste is not very stringent about this, and there is absolutely no comparison between her and government agencies on this policy. The hell people go through getting food stamps and other benefits is totally at the other end of the spectrum from the way Celeste works. And she is tough and angry and speaks *very* candidly about what she thinks of those books of rules and regulations and forms *they* make you fill out. She'll take no government money; she wants none of their rules. *Dignity* is her rule, *human dignity*, and no one is going to get a run-around at Gleaners in Las Vegas.

People may pay for the food if they want to do so. She averages 25 cents per family member, but it is important that they pay whatever they can....It preserves their dignity. Rules and regulations: because she and federal agencies totally disagree on how to feed people, the government refuses to cash $7,000 worth of food stamps sitting in her safe. People had paid for some of their food with these coupons, and she takes them, though there won't be any return on their value.

People may volunteer to work certain hours at the food bank...another dignity-preserver. One older woman who used to always complain about her bad heart and other medical problems no longer does has time or the desire to complain. She has too many other things of great import on her agenda to worry about those things. She has people to help feed.

And people have come in and literally fainted from hunger while they were picking out their food, this food that would have been thrown in the dumpsters: produce perhaps slightly damaged, cans and jars and containers with expiration dates that have passed but still legal for Celeste to use — and eminently edible.

All the food is donated.

And when I ask if any of those who come to Gleaners are Jewish, she doesn't miss a beat. "Yes, of course."

And when I ask — following the old myth that most Jewish people living in poverty are elderly — when I ask if these Jewish people are all elderly, she answers (never missing a beat), "Of course not." (Gleaners has kosher meats, too.)

And next door they've got about a half-dozen homeless people sheltered, tied in with some other program Celeste is involved in. I have come to expect that.

HOW MUCH FOOD

I want to return to the scene at the warehouse.

The room is *so* huge, bigger than anything I would have possibly imagined. 40-some-thousand square feet. The sheer number of pounds of food is over-whelming. (I must have seen 1,000 loaves of bread on the racks.) Jars and jars and cans and cans and packages and packages on pallets and shelves and stacked up everywhere.

And there is a network of Gleaners food banks around the country, well over 100 of them, and they often swap supplies, to the tune of 10-20,000 pound shipments at a time. So if one Gleaners is short of a particular item, and another has an abundance of that item, off goes a truck with 15,000 pounds of food which will most certainly reach the hungry people immediately.

15,000 pounds here, another 20,000 pounds there. So much food!

There's also two resident cats, very happy cats. So there are no mice.

(And the cats don't mess with Precious.)

EXACTLY WHY CELESTE DOES WHAT SHE DOES

Celeste gave me a videotape of a number of local and national newsclips that had been done about Gleaners. Two things stand out in one of the clips that I like to show at my programs: one is a brief statement by a young woman who has come to Gleaners to get food. She says, "Here they encourage you to take as much as you need". The other thing that excites me is a morning prayer-circle. I am usually wary of the thinly veiled religious fanaticism when it comes to feeding, cloth-ing, and housing people in need. On occasion I have come to suspect that some of the people providing these things are more out to win souls for their brand of reli-gion than to benefit the people who are hungry and cold and homeless.

Not so with Celeste's prayer-circle. At the beginning of each day Celeste invites one of the volunteers to recite a prayer — it could be a Catholic or Protestant prayer, a Jewish one, or a free-form personal word. The prayer on this particular video was free-form, but as soon as the prayer was finished, Celeste says something like, "All right, let's get to work." For her, prayer *has* to lead to action.

Celeste has no vested interest in the souls of the people she feeds. She just personally feels that she is in partnership with God, doing divine (yet human) work on the Lord's behalf. No fanatic this one; by no means is she out to win souls.

It *is* true that she put God on her Board of Directors. In fact, when the Gleaners stationery was being printed, the printer wanted to know if she was certain that's the way she wanted it, with God's name right there on the paper, at the top of the list. That's how she wanted it. I like that. I like that because she is in the habit of saying, "The more you hoard, the less you have; the more you give away, the more there is."

CELESTE HERSELF

Celeste McKinley used to be an entertainer, a singer and comedian who played the clubs. She was also a successful businesswoman in Las Vegas, at one time owning two businesses that were doing very well. As she changed over to this other world of Gleaners, there were sacrifices. She gave up the businesses, and only recently got her jewelry out of the pawn shop. She almost lost her house on a number of occasions.

She and David lived on $6,000 last year (though there is an abundance of food, of course.) They don't really need much in the way of dollars, David and Celeste.

They seem like two of the happiest people in the world.

JOSEPH LORDI

About a week after meeting Celeste in Las Vegas, I was in Youngstown, Ohio, for a program. I had asked her about the other branches of Gleaners around the country, and she said she knew a few of the directors personally and some more through the mail and from phone calls. She particularly praised Joseph Lordi in Youngstown.

As it happened, the Youngstown connection slipped my mind, and I was already through the early program and a couple of hours away from the evening's events with the community's Jewish leadership when I remembered about Joseph.

David, Precious and Celeste McKinley.

Joseph Lordi at his Youngstown Community Food Center.

I called Celeste and asked her to track him down and to ask him if he could come out to the program that evening.

Fortunately, Celeste made the connection and Joseph appeared.

During the program, I asked him to say a few words — maybe five or ten minutes — about The Youngstown Community Food Center and Gleaners Food Bank. He spoke quietly, in sharp contrast to my hellfire and brimstone style, but everyone was moved, very moved. Joseph's food bank feeds 300 people a day and he is still in the early stages of locating an appropriate facility as the volumes of food and numbers of hungry people who come to his Gleaners grow.

Joseph's "story" is different from Celeste's, not quite the serendipitous food-for-the-cockatoo tale that she had told me. The fact is that Joseph had been in the food industry for 18 years, and he and his brothers had a grocery store of their own for a while, but it failed. He went through his savings and wound up on the public assistance rolls where he received humiliating treatment. Forms and documentation and insensitive workers beat him down. For 18 months he was unemployed. It was at that point, realizing the strain on himself and his family, that Joseph decided to change the way people in Youngstown who needed food should get it.

Joseph had seen a story about Celeste's food bank on "60 Minutes". He took one of his welfare checks, bought a ticket for Las Vegas to see her in action, and then came back and started his own Gleaners. He had learned from the expert-of-experts, and it was obvious that they absolutely agreed on the most basic of all principles: dignity. As with Celeste's operation, all the food was donated by grocery stores, food distributors, manufacturers, and private individuals. And as with his teacher's operation, the food is free. And as with Gleaners of Las Vegas, people do not stand in line and get pre-packaged packages. They shop just like anyone else who shops for groceries.

When Joseph had finished speaking, what struck us all was his quality of innocence and simplicity; these qualities are called in Hebrew "Temimut". He is so gentle and unassuming. I believe those qualities form the basis for his work. He had been treated badly, and that was not the way things *had* to be. He, Joseph Lordi, would set out to do it right.

It was all so simple. The day-to-day worries of running a food bank are never so simple. But the *fact* of it is.

And he is, indeed, doing it right.

And many hungry people are not so hungry any more in Youngstown, Ohio.

Joseph Lordi, Youngstown Community Food Center, Inc., and Gleaners Food Bank, POB 3587, Boardman OH 44513. Phone 216-726-9591.

ALICE MOSINIAK

Six weeks after meeting Joseph in Youngstown I was back in Ohio, this time in Toledo for four days of community programs. Again, it slipped my mind — was there a Gleaners or some similar program out that way, and some heroic figure behind it all? During one of those four days I remembered, called Celeste, and she gave me a name: Alice Mosiniak.

Let's get the suspense out of the way.

Alice Mosiniak is 65 years old and handles 1,000,000 pounds of food a month for twenty counties in Ohio. She came to one of the programs and spoke, as Joseph had done in Youngstown. (Celeste and David preferred just to sit quietly in the back when I was in Las Vegas, but when I introduced them to the audience, it generated a lot of volunteers and other assistance afterwards.)

There were about forty people at the program that evening, Jewish leaders, and we were all stunned by what we heard. I had expected that, but even when you expect to be dazzled and overwhelmed, it is still a powerful experience. There is nothing boring to it.

I asked Alice to repeat that incredible number — 1,000,000 pounds of food a month — so it would sink in. Afterwards, people responded with offers to work with her. That, too, thankfully, is something I have come to expect.

But it was that 1,000,000 pounds of food I kept coming back to. Alix Greenblatt, who had arranged everything for my trip, and I set a time to meet Alice down at the Toledo Seagate Food Bank one morning. We had to see what this number was in real life, with our own eyes. What we saw was so overpowering it is still hard to believe that somewhere in Toledo, Ohio, is all this food that is being saved from the garbage, perfectly good food, and given at no cost to people who are downright hungry.

There were rooms and rooms and freezers and storage spaces with stacks and stacks of food. At one point I stopped Alice and asked (motioning with my arm), "From here to there, how much cheese is that?" "35,000 pounds." One of the freezers seemed to go on forever. An elderly man was working away going through bushels of potatoes to separate the good ones from the bad. And on the second or third floor of the warehouse there was a young college kid, home on break for a few weeks, moving boxes with a handtruck and carrying cartons and cartons of soup and other canned goods.

I had to stop this person and ask him about his work. I had to ask him why he was doing it, but, as soon as I asked I knew what he would answer. It was something like, "This is what I should be doing." It was another in a long series of refreshing revelations that morning. I could pile on the details, but the essential fact is clear: through good will, hard effort, and a true, deep sense of caring, 1,000,000 pounds of food gets moved each month through Alice's network to the tables and refrigerators and freezers of thousands of hungry people.

These are facts and figures, if one can estimate them at all, that have come along with my explorations into the world of food and hunger:

1. Celeste says that the amount of food thrown out in this country annually is worth $27,000,000,000.

2. Another article I read put it at $31,000,000,000.

3. Celeste says that there is enough food thrown out to feed 47,000,000 hungry people.

4. Dr. J. Larry Brown estimates that there are 20,000,000 hungry people in America.

I don't think anyone can give accurate figures, but even rounding off and estimating roughly, the conclusions that we could reach should be clear: moving the food from the store to hungry people (and not to the dumpster) would solve so much of the problem. Not all of it, that is certain. And, I would have to stress that you would need Celeste McKinleys and Joseph Lordis and Alice Mosiniaks to handle the food. In some places food banking has become big business, and some people make an all right living from it, perhaps more than all right. There are a few (*but not many*) shady sides to this work, and, *on rare occasions* there might be some unpleasantries and unethical practices. But not with Celeste and Joseph and Alice. They're in it for the pure Mitzvah of it all. Because it isn't just food. It's people; it's human dignity.

I joked with Alice on the phone yesterday. I told her I was going to write that she wasn't ready to retire yet. She laughed and said it was all right.

Alice isn't ready to retire just yet. There is still too much to be done.

Alice Mosiniak, Toledo Seagate Food Bank, 526 High St., Toledo, OH 43609, 419-244-6996.

People lined up for the 800 family distributions.   Alice Mosiniak.

REFLECTIONS IV

A certain 17-year-old from the New York area named Stephen Katz started a Mitzvah project called G.I.F.T., which stands for Generous Intentions Feel Terrific. He and his friend, Mike Gerber, gathered some 2,000 items and delivered them to various shelters in Manhattan.

Then something went wrong.

He applied to a number of colleges, and showed a particular interest in getting into Vassar. What went wrong was his interview.

The interviewer was a college senior, who (as the article I read says) "either gave Stephen a taste of how the cold cruel world really sees people like Stephen Katz, or gave him his first taste of the gamesmanship that passes for intellectual debate in academia".

The interviewer, this fourth-year student at Vassar, asked Stephen what he was up to. Stephen, naturally enough, told him about G.I.F.T.

Then all hell broke loose. As Stephen recalls the conversation, the interviewer reacted by saying, "Do you think that's really practical? Aren't you just prolonging their suffering?" Stephen remembers that the college senior (with more than 3 years of wisdom under his belt) then began to talk about Social Darwinism and other such theories of society.

An argument ensued.

Stephen felt disappointed. He thought he might have wrecked his chances for Vassar, concluding, "I don't think I did too well."

The fact is, he did wonderfully well.

The Vassar genius blew it.

TREVOR FERRELL

This is a story to feel good about:

I don't know whether or not it was a cold night in Philadelphia on December 8, 1983. I haven't checked the moon charts to see if it was dark, and I haven't dug up an old copy of the *Inquirer, so* I can't really say whether or not it was snowing, but the local TV news had a story that night about the city's homeless people.

Out in the suburbs, in a large house with a pool in the back, an 11-year-old kid named Trevor Ferrell happened to see the newsclip. It's been over three decades since I was eleven years old, and I can't remember very well what kinds of things I thought about at that age, but something moved Trevor to ask his father if they could go down and see the people who live on the street.

You may use big words like "revelation" or "epiphany" if you want to, but I would rather think Trevor was only mildly curious about the news report...perhaps a little more than "mildly curious", but still just curious. And surprized. That much I know, because I have met many suburban kids in the '70's and '80's who by Trevor's age certainly have had no real contact with homeless people, and wouldn't suspect that they live near them. It's a psychological and human defense, and a good one in the most positive sense: if human beings tried to absorb all the pain in the world — near and far — and feel it as if it were nearby and immediate, it might drive them over the edge. (A teacher named Abba Binyamin said it centuries ago in the Talmud, "If the eye only had the power to see, human beings could not handle all the Evil Things, so overpowering is the weight and sum of it all." [Brachot 6a])

So I prefer to think that Trevor was merely curious. And it appears he must have been very insistent. His father, Frank, agreed to take him down to see some of Philadelphia's homeless people, but when he agreed he meant "in a few days" or "next week". This was, after all, an unusual request from an 11-year-old boy. But Trevor pushed; Father and Son went back and forth, maybe even arguing. Finally, Frank gave in, and Trevor, Frank, Janet — Trevor's mother — and one or two of the other Ferrell children got into the car and drove down to see the street people.

I am writing this before 7:00 a.m. and it's too early to call the Ferrells to get more details. So it's hard to say if after — a half-hour ride into Center City — they spent 10 minutes or 45 minutes or 28 minutes searching the streets before they found a "real-live" homeless person. I would think they had a basic idea where to locate people who live in alleyways and sleep on grates, but to know *exactly* where they might be is another matter.

It's too early to call and ask if — after finding the first one — they spent another 5 minutes or 24 minutes or hour and a half driving around looking for others. There is one fact, though, that everyone who knows Trevor knows: he had taken a blanket with him from back home.

The Ferrells locked the car doors when they got down to Center City. You do it, and I do it, and there is good reason to lock the doors, particularly when riding with children in certain places. But somewhere on their drive around the streets, they must have stopped the car for a moment. Trevor unlocked his door before Frank or Janet knew what was happening, stepped out of the car with blanket in hand, walked up to one of the people, and handed it to him. Trevor was innocent (we'll come back to that) and unafraid.

As the Ferrells tell it, the man who received the blanket was very appreciative. They were very moved by the man's reaction, and on the ride back to their home in Gladwyne spoke about their experience.

The next night they went back to the streets again, this time with some food, and the next night they went again, and the night after, and the night after that...every night until at least last night, May 5, 1988. And I assume they will be back again tonight and tomorrow night and the night after that, too. Most of the time it's some member or two of the Ferrell family and a number of the volunteers who have joined Trevor's Campaign for the Homeless.

These are my most recent statistics: they have fed over 180,000 meals to homeless individuals. And Trevor's Gang has never missed a night on the streets. Rain, snow, sleet, whatever. Never. (There will be more statistics later.) What happened in the interim is that the media took hold of this "hot story", and within six months, Trevor's name was in headlines around the country, on the TV news as news items and special segments. And someone wrote *Trevor's Place*, a book (a *must read* book) about what Trevor and his Gang were doing. It was The Media at Its Best.

As a result of all the publicity, people came to help Trevor and the family, all kinds of people: rich people and poor people and people in between; old people and young people and people somewhere in the middle; suburban folks and people who worked and/or lived in Center City and people from towns an hour or more away; individuals who couldn't see and others who could; and people with problems and people who are without problems; and fancy law firms (like Dechert Price and Rhoades) and builders; and teachers with their schoolchildren, Christians and Jews; and, I would suspect, doubters and fanatics of every sort, too. Many came, and still come, because people who are hungry and cold would be without food and warmth without their efforts. Others came because *they themselves* probably needed it as much as the people on the street, but, once having ridden with "Trevor's Gang", they grew, and now do it because of the needs of the people on the street.

I fall into some of those categories: a suburban writer, living 120 miles away from Philadelphia, Jewish and a sometimes religious skeptic, neither young nor particularly old, not particularly normal, not quite sure whether I was coming totally for the benefit of the street people. In that last phrase is a tricky aspect of all Tzedakah work: are we (1) doing it for those who need it, (2) are we doing it for ourselves, or (3) are we doing it for other people, and, along the way, we manage to reap many benefits because of the nature of Mitzvahs. In that third category, I think it is fair to say that I wanted to be with Trevor to see if I could re-capture some of my childhood innocence, though I am still trying to understand all three of the categories and exactly how I fit in.

FIRST VISIT

Here I was, reading articles about The Kid, wanting to meet him and see him in action. As it happened, I had a speaking engagement for one Winter morning in Philadelphia, and I decided to take the train in the night before. I called the Ferrells and arranged to meet them at Trevor's Place, the shelter they have established. I also made sure that my old friend and host for the night, Marty Millison, would meet me down at the shelter so I wouldn't be alone. I was, quite candidly, scared, even though I always talked a good game of doing this kind of Mitzvah work....I was really putting myself on the line.

I took a 10-minute cab ride from 30th Street Station, to the address Frank and Janet had given me. This *was* a snowy, cold night, and I was saying to myself in the cab, "I hope Trevor or Marty gets there before I do." I didn't know what I would do if I got there first and would have to walk inside the shelter alone among the people Trevor has taken in. I didn't really know how to talk to "them" and listen to "them" (it was still "them" and "me" back then).

I have to backtrack.

The shelter, Trevor's Place. Somewhere along the way as the word began to spread about Trevor, a woman named Mother Divine (widow of Father Divine), gave Trevor a run-down building they could use for a shelter. (I just called Frank and Janet. They say that things happened so quickly that it was February, 1984, when the building was given to them — only two months after they had begun their work — and by March 18th it was opened. That's about the 100th day of Trevor's Campaign.)

In those days Trevor's Place was a wreck. It violated so many building and health codes, I am not exactly sure why the city let them keep it open so long. A couple of years later it was closed, massive renovations were done, and it is now open again, with a capacity for about 50 people. As of the Spring of 1988, they have managed to find permanent housing for 84% of the people who come into the shelter, and 80% of the people of Trevor's Place have found jobs.

Returning now to the cold, snowy night when I went to see Trevor and the family — Trevor and Frank did, in fact, get there before me. When I stepped out of the cab, I looked into the window and saw Trevor standing in one of the big rooms hugging one of his friends, one of the people who otherwise would have been out on the streets. The scene was very moving, and, while it did not do away with all of my apprehensions, it certainly made things easier for me.

When I went inside, I noticed a few things right away. It was inordinately hot. It felt like the thermostat must have been set at around 80 degrees. Later on, I would theorize that, if you have lived on the streets and have a very real fear of the cold and of freezing to death — and when an alternative to the streets presents itself — you want to make *absolutely* sure you are going to be warm. But those thoughts were for a later time; at that moment when I came into the shelter, the heat blasted me. I recently read another article from the *Washington Post* that said that in the Winter of 1987-88, 13 people froze to death in Washington, most of them on the streets. When I finished the article, the issue of the heat made more sense to me.

As soon as I came in and met Frank and Trevor I also noticed that The Kid is quiet, even shy (except with His People). I don't know what I had expected, but I had somehow imagined he would be a high-powered dynamo shuffling schedules and contractors and meal plans and forms for getting government assistance. I knew what he looked like from the pictures in the newspapers, but I was surprized and enthralled that he was so quiet and low-key. And innocent.

Trevor was about 13 at the time, a little taller than the earliest pictures of him on the streets, and I am sure this "Kidness" appealed to hundreds of people who volunteered to work with him. And he was cute (in real life and particularly from some of the early photographs of him that I've seen)...in his "braces-years". There was something obviously surrealistic about the scene. Here's a kid in braces, and there's a bunch of people from the streets. And here's the kid hugging them and talking to them and playing with their kids and in low-key manner taking me on a tour of the building and introducing me to the people, his friends, and showing me a private room of one of the people he has taken in. As natural and normal as could be.

Within a few minutes, this innocence and naturalness had set me at ease. Later on, as I would think about my time with Trevor and the family, I would begin to develop talks for my audiences about normalcy. Trevor had taught me — among many, many other things — that it *can be* perfectly normal to be a Kid and to feed, clothe, and house homeless people, and maybe that it *should be* normal to do such things, and that maybe kids of all ages who don't yet do it might not be "normal"...at least not yet.

I took the tour, talked with Trevor and Frank, slept at Marty's, and gave my speech the next day. The talk I had thought to give had been radically changed, and Trevor and his work became a central part of it all. My speeches have changed even more since then, and I often show a video of Trevor at work, and I sell the book and the video wherever I go, and I encourage people to ride into Philadelphia to see it all for themselves.

Other things have changed, too. Trevor is now 15, and six feet tall. He's no longer cute, just gorgeous. I am told by the Proud Mother Janet that when he goes on the road to speak they practically need to call the police to keep the drooling teen-age girls off of him.

What hasn't changed is this: Trevor is still Trevor. Many people fear that all of this work and subsequent fame has warped him, scarred him...."Where does he go from here, famous so young?" People ask me about that, but my friend Joel

Grishaver in Los Angeles said that when Trevor was out there, after they worked the streets (naturally), Joel, Trevor, and Frank wanted to go to a movie — Trevor's choice. He wanted to see "The Fly", a rather gross movie I might have liked when I was 13 or 14, but not really to my taste at this stage of life. What would we expect? An avant garde film? A foreign, brooding, philosophical flick? No, "The Fly" it was.

At one later date, when Frank and Trevor and Janet came out to one of my programs in Philadelphia, someone asked him how all this had affected him. There he was, nearly six feet tall, into his 15th year of life, answering, "I'm still the same kid."

That says it all.

SECOND VISIT

I still hadn't ridden with Trevor and the Gang on their nightly circuit. It was one thing to go to the shelter and see the street people as former street people in a controlled setting of a shelter. These were mostly people who were working hard at getting into a real home, getting employment, getting on their feet, starting again, and for some, starting all over again. They could stay as long as they needed to at Trevor's Place; it was their home, and they were safe from the dangers of street life, protected by Trevor Ferrell and his Gang. But it was something entirely different — my risking going out on the streets to feed them — searching around dark corners of buildings and on heating grates.

People ask Trevor, "Weren't you afraid?" No, he wasn't afraid, though I believe there is reason to be afraid in many places. You don't just go out on the street in certain parts of town and go up to a stranger who might be down on his or her luck and give out blankets and food and coffee or juice. I don't think I would have done it in Washington, but in Philadelphia it was safe. Trevor had a protective shield around him. He was the friend of the people who lived on the streets. They respected him, loved him, would do anything to make sure he was safe and happy. (One of Trevor's friends, Chico, puts it this way, "Anybody try to hurt that boy, they gotta walk through me. And that's the truth.")

I went into Philadelphia in September, 1987, and I wasn't quite so afraid. First, I was under Trevor's protection, and second, he had helped dispel the myth that such a high percentage of the homeless are supposed to be mentally ill. (A few months later I would see an article in the *The New York Times* that summarized a survey done by the New York Psychiatric Institute. They studied the population of homeless people in the city's shelters, and the conclusions were that 37% of them could live entirely on their own, another 37% could live independently with some support, and the remaining quarter of the shelter residents needed various levels of supervision, 10% being the most serious, needing 24-hour-a-day supervision or psychiatric hospitalization.)

So I went back to Philadelphia somewhat apprehensive, but not as much as I would have been had I not visited Trevor's Place a few months before. Frank picked me up in the van that says "Trevor's Campaign" and we went back to their house for a while before beginning the nightly run. (One of the vans is leased to them for $1.00 a year by a local dealership.) It's a nice house in a nice neighborhood, though it is clear the Ferrells have neglected it somewhat. The front door needs painting, the lawn needs better care, and other things are noticeable. But I'm sure they will get around to these things "someday". For now, though, they're a little too tied up to worry about the door and the lawn.

I met Trevor's mother, Janet, and his younger sister, Jody, age 11. Later that night I would meet Allen, Trevor's older brother. (Trevor's other sister, Liza, is a junior in college in Boston). We talked for a while, loaded the van with food, and then six of us (three Ferrells, me, and two volunteers from a church about an hour up the road) headed for Center City. It was warm and a little muggy, about 75 degrees outside.

Nowadays Trevor's Campaign has two or three regular stops before they start combing the streets for individuals. At the first stop there were about 40 people who gathered around the van, and all the Ferrells were recognized, greeted, and the friendly, dignified process of feeding casseroles and juice to the people in line began. Trevor asked if I wanted to dish out the food from the back, but I was still hesitant (though unafraid), and said I'd do the juice from the side. So the people would first go to Trevor and get their food, then come to me. I overheard some people say how hungry they were; I heard the recurring phrase Trevor's Gang hears night after night, "Can I have seconds?" I kept glancing back at Trevor and kept Janet close by, but I had loosened up. I began to see just how natural and easy this Mitzvah was.

There were no fistfights, there was no tension in the air, no pushing or shoving. These were not "bums". In fact, I don't think I ever heard the Ferrells use the word "bums". As a kid I remember thinking of bums when we'd go to Griffith Stadium, the old Washington baseball field where the Senators played. It wasn't a good neighborhood, and there were a number of people around who looked like what some people would call "bums". But I don't feel comfortable with that word any more. Trevor has reminded us that they are "people", not "bums".

When we finished the first stop, Frank became worried we would run out of food. It happens now and again. We decided to go to the nearby Wendy's to see what could be arranged. Frank went to the counter and ordered 25 orders of chili, which took the Wendy's person a little by surprise (as was to be expected). He asked to speak to the manager, and when Frank identified himself and offered to pay, the young woman in charge of the restaurant responded with the same spirit that so many others have shown: she filled the big jug with lemonade for free and gave us about 40 or 50 portions of chili, charging us for about 20 of them. She even loaned us the big pot.

It was a fine moment for all of us. Fewer people would go hungry that night.

After loading the pot of chili into the van, we headed out for the second stop, fed those people (by now I was ready to serve the food), and started to comb the many streets the Ferrells knew so well. They spotted individuals in the alleys and in the open, on side streets and in parts of Center City which, during the day, are the places where "regular life" goes on with businesses and offices and restaurants and travel agencies, streets Philadelphians know well: Walnut and Spruce and Market, the middle of Center City. We also covered out-of-the-way places, too, but I was struck the next morning when I went back downtown. The night before it had been such a different world.

These are some of the things that happened as we made "Grand Rounds":

At one point Trevor showed me a slanted grate, angled such that people could not sleep on them and gain the benefit of the warm air coming up from the building's heating.

At another time Trevor asked, "Do you want to take care of that person?" I took a deep breath, decided to grow up a little, opened the van door, and walked out to the street where a young white woman, perhaps 20 years old, sat on some cloth bags that looked like carry-on luggage for an airplane. I suppose that she had all her worldly possessions in those bags. She seemed distant, spacey. I approached and asked if she was hungry. She said she wasn't. I asked if she wanted some lemonade, and she said, "Yes." I brought her over to the van, gave her some lemonade, walked her back to her bags, and then we drove off. The Ferrells took note of who she was. (They told me they had seen many, many young people — and little kids, of course. The Ferrells worked with one young person who used to ride public transportation all night. For two years they worked with her. She is now a pre-medical student at the University of Pennsylvania.)

A little later Trevor sent me out again, this time to an elderly black man who was sitting on a street corner. Next to him, lying on a grate, was a piece of white bread. I went up to him and put my hand on his shoulder (which astounded me, and still astounds me; I am still growing up; you feed the street people, you shelter them and give them blankets, but you don't *touch* them, or so I thought, until that moment). I told him who we were, and asked if he wanted something to eat. He turned his head towards me, and said "Yes", and I saw that he was blind. I brought over some chili and lemonade, said what Trevor always says, "God bless you", and went back to the van to continue the circuit.

At various times people would approach the van and ask if there were any blankets. It was September, and very warm, and I thought Winter was a long way off. Our seasonal timeclock is much different than that of the people who live on the streets.

There was a certain joy in the work, and a lot of joking around which eased some of the tension. Trevor's good at that — joking around — not because it's good therapy, but because that's the way he is. I kept asking the Ferrells more and more questions. Enthusiasm and an incredible sense of caring pervaded the conversation. I did not find it depressing, not in the least, because something immediate was being done: hungry people were being fed and their spirits were being raised at every turn.

And occasionally, as we drove around, people would honk their horns. At first I thought it was because Frank was such a bad driver, which *is* a fact, but the Ferrells explained that people driving around the streets recognize Trevor's van and want to make contact. They honk, sometimes pulling up at a traffic light and handing them a contribution. Frank says a cop even pulled them over once. He was sure he was going to get a ticket. But the policeman only wanted to give them a contribution.

Later, we would go out for pizza, and the Ferrells would help me gather my thoughts. As was to be expected, back at the house Trevor gave up his room for me. It was a nice room, though a little too teen-agey with too many glaring posters of teen-ager-type heroes on the walls.

In the morning Frank got me a ride back to Center City for some business I had to do. My life was supposedly returning to normal.

A GATHERING OF SCATTERED FACTS: THINGS YOU MIGHT STILL WANT TO KNOW ABOUT TREVOR AND HIS FAMILY

Trevor has been showered with honors throughout the United States. But he's not a publicity-seeker nor one who runs after honors. No one in the family is out there to become famous. The Ferrells are so honest and straightforward and incorruptible that it takes very little time before recognizing that they are doing this because it is what has to be done. They're certainly not in it for personal gain.

Trevor's been to Calcutta twice to see and work with Mother Teresa.

His record for largest audience addressed: 6,000 people, kids out in Colorado.

In the beginning, as Trevor began to get publicity for his work, some of his friends at school made fun of him. Here he was, an 11-year-old boy getting national publicity for feeding the homeless. Perhaps they thought he was a bit of a freak. Soon, though, they joined him.

Trevor failed public speaking in school. He talks quietly and, compared to some fiery speakers on the lecture circuit, he could be very boring. He usually speaks for a few minutes and then invites questions. But no one is bored, and the style of delivery really doesn't matter very much. It's who Trevor is that counts, and no matter how dead-pan the presentation is, people want to listen.

Trevor is learning-disabled, dyslexic. So is his brother, Allen, as is Frank. In fact, Trevor is now in a very small special school in Massachusetts doing fabulously well in his studies. (His brother has a fistful of acceptances at fine colleges.) When he's home from school he's back on the streets, and while he's away, the family and the large company of volunteers carry on the work. Trevor- just-being-

Trevor has taught me so much about being achievement-oriented. He has made me re-think what the authentic achievements in life really are.

The Kid knows failure from his academic record in school, from the people who occasionally refuse the food he offers them, from the ones he helps get off the street and who slide back out into homelessness. He's certainly not naive about the realities, the need for funding (and the family is not particularly good at raising funds), the problems with running and getting enough supplies for their thrift shop, the worries about having enough food to feed people, and paying the salaries of resident counsellors at Trevor's Place.

Those are harsh realities, and Trevor knows them well. But at the end of one of the videotapes Trevor says, "I am only one, but still I am one. I cannot do everything, but still I can do something. And because I can't do everything, I will not refuse to do something I can do." It sounds like it's right out of an ancient Jewish text, *Sayings of Our Ancestors (Pirke Avot)*, and if someone else had said it, it might ring false. But it is Trevor speaking, and it makes sense.

Here's a nice note from Trevor's Spring 1985, newsletter that will articulate his thinking better:

> *I would like to thank you for your help and I hope you will continue. This past month has been exciting. I met the President in Washington, Brother Joe Ranieri who helps the homeless in Florida and Darrell Gilliam who helps the homeless in Oklahoma.*
>
> *A lot of people have been concerned about my school grades. Well, things are going fine. I have been trying harder and I am getting all A's and B's. On Spring break I went to Disney World and had a great good time.*
>
> *I am glad that winter is over. One night my dad and I tried to sleep on the street, but it was so cold we couldn't do it. We lasted only 3 hours. I don't know how my friends on the street do it.*

Nice and straight. Just what you'd expect from a normal 13-year-old (at that time) kid.

The Ferrells are churchgoing people. They go to a Presbyterian church in their community, but they're not fanatics, and they are not evangelical. They don't try to impose any kind of Christianity on you, but I have seen from them what Christian can mean in its highest sense.

Frank explained that they used to hear and talk about charity on Sunday mornings, and now they were doing what they had talked about for so long. In our many talks about the Jewish idea of Tzedek and Tzedakah as Justice and Righ-

The Ferrells at home. Clockwise from Janet (seated in chair), Jody, Trevor, Liza, Allen and Frank.

teousness, it is apparent that the love element merges comfortably with Tzedek and Tzedakah. They are — to whatever extent they are able — setting aright some things that are just plain wrong in this world

Frank closed up his electronics store a while back and they live off of some grants from the foundation...hardly an enormous salary. They were better off financially before. And I wouldn't lie to you that there aren't family tensions, normal ones and ones that have become worse because of Trevor's Campaign. There are strains; yes, there are tensions, and personal needs that get overridden because a van breaks down or because a volunteer can't make it one night or because the cost of fixing up Trevor's Place is so overwhelming. It's a rosy picture, but not all rosy.

But the videos and newsclips and newspaper and magazine articles that tell Trevor's story are all true. Don't doubt them for a minute.

SOMETHING THAT RECENTLY SHOOK ME

I was doing a talk about Tzedakah with a group of teen-agers. One of them remarked something to the effect that there will always be the same number of hungry and homeless people out there. I was taken aback, and I realized I had lost perspective because of my age. Many teen-agers see life differently because they were born at a certain time in American history.

I have talked to my parents about the bread lines and soup kitchens and unemployment in The Great Depression. I know Dorothea Lange's and Margaret Bourke-White's and Walker Evans's famous photographs from that period of American history, the sharecroppers and Dust Bowl victims and the migrants Woody Guthrie sang about. That was more than 50 years ago, in my parents' growing-up years. My own parallel years in the 1950's and 1960's certainly never experienced such an all-pervading calamity. Now the 1980's have been much worse than when I was a teen-ager and in my early twenties. I can't imagine what these teen-agers — products of the 1980's — feel, what makes them feel and think that what we have now is what we will always have.

I know it won't *always* be that way; I just *know* it.

Trevor assures us that it simply won't always be the way it is now.

If you want to see the world differently, ride the van, see Trevor's Place. If you want to be so sure about things like this, meet Trevor, his family, and the rest of the Gang.

Trevor's Campaign, Box 21, Gladwyne PA 19035. Phone: 215-325-0640 or 1-800-TREVORS.

REFLECTIONS V

In the First Century of the Common Era, a certain Queen Helena and her son, Monobaz, converted to Judaism. The kingdom was called Adiabene, in what is now modern-day Iraq. Monobaz (or Munbaz, as he is known in the ancient Jewish texts) eventually succeeded his father, Monobaz I, to the throne, and a number of wonderful stories about the royal mother and son are related in the Talmud. One such story about Munbaz II is a Grand Tale of Tzedakah:

At a certain point in his life, King Munbaz gave away all of his wealth to the poor. His relatives complained to him, saying, "The generation before you accumulated even greater treasures than their ancestors. Now see what you have done! You have wasted both your own wealth and that of your ancestors!"

King Munbaz replied, "I have outdone them all.

"My ancestors accumulated earthly things; I have gathered things for Heaven....

"My ancestors saved money that did not pay dividends; my money is paying dividends....

"My ancestors stored things that could be stolen; mine can't be stolen....

"My ancestors amassed money; I have collected souls....

"My ancestors hoarded things that wound up in the possession of other people; what I have done will always be mine...." (Jerusalem Talmud, Pe'ah 1:1)

Munbaz's words are very admirable. He articulates a most eloquent perspective on the essences of Tzedakah.

However, there is a slightly different version in the Babylonian Talmud (Bava Batra 11a). In that version, the text states that Munbaz did his great Mitzvah when a terrible drought had devastated the country.

The two sources represent two different kinds of giving: in the latter version, Munbaz's Mitzvah was prompted by an immediate need — catastrophe was imminent. In the former text, where there was no specific disaster to stimulate his conscience, he must have reached a heightened level of awareness in his own mind and set out to initiate a new, more intensified pattern of giving Tzedakah. Both approaches are still evident in today's world.

One commentator points out that, since Jewish tradition sets an upper limit of 20% of one's income for Tzedakah, the added detail about the drought must be the more accurate historical source. In situations of extreme human danger, the 20% upper limit may be suspended. Thus the extent of Munbaz's dazzling act of Tzedakah.

URI LUPOLIANSKY

A sure sign of a Mitzvah project's success is that whenever someone can't solve a problem, they say "Call So-and-So" or "Go over to and talk to X". This is the case with Uri Lupoliansky and his Mitzvah work at Yad Sarah, the project that lends out medical equipment for free to anyone who needs it. People from all sectors of Israeli society send people to Yad Sarah. Everyone who is anyone, and many, many people who are no-one-in-particular knows Yad Sarah. The only ones who *don't* know are the ones who are sent there by people who *do* know. *All of them* are confident that Uri and Yad Sarah will be able to solve their various problems.

Uri and Yad Sarah must be *very* successful, judging by how often this referral process happens. Because the project is so simple and straightforward, it is not difficult to understand why so many people end up on the phone with Uri or find themselves in his office on HaNevi'im Street in Jerusalem.

I'm drawing a blank this morning....I can't seem to recall how I first found Uri. It wasn't my Mother; I told *her* about this Mitzvah hero.

It might have been some newspaper article, or possibly one of my friends in Jerusalem who scans the human horizon, on the look-out for new people for me to meet. Reviewing old annual Tzedakah reports that I send out to my contributors, I see that Yad Sarah first appears in 1979 when it was in its third year of operation. At that time it had 18 lending stations in Israel. As of April 1, 1988 it has 56 stations. In fact, moving into its 12th year, Yad Sarah has some fairly staggering statistics:

1. 3,270 volunteers
2. 19 1/3 salaries (Israeli salaries go by whole, half, quarter, and thirds)
3. 56 lending stations (as I just mentioned)
4. 11,600 wheelchairs
5. 1,600 glucometers for diabetics
6. 80 portable oxygen machines
7. Nearly uncountable thousands of other pieces of equipment of almost every shape, purpose, and kind imaginable.

But I am ahead of myself. We should start with Uri. Uri is younger than I am, in his mid-to-late 30's, a kid. Since I am now 43 years old, I often consider people younger than I am "just a kid", even if they are 37 or so, like Uri. He is the father of 10 or 11 children (I lost track).

Uri's father founded Yad Sarah 11 years ago, and when his father passed away, Uri became the director. Moving backward in time, that means he became Yad Sarah's director when he was in his mid 20's.

Uri is an orthodox Jew. He wears a head covering, usually a traditional Yarmulka that many religious Jews wear, and sometimes a black fedora. He wears basic black suits (or sometimes a sweater in Winter), a white shirt, and a tie, though the jacket is very often draped over the back of his chair and the tie loosened. And, yes, he has a beard. It's not a full-face beard, but rather one that goes around the rim of his face. He does not look particularly prophetic, or otherworldly or particularly visionary. Most important of all about his appearance: he looks gentle.

This gentle look throws you off balance the first time you meet him. You would expect that the director of such a Mitzvah project would be thunderous or imposing or at least august. As he sees himself, so he appears to others: one Jew doing for others what has to be done. I will say this again later. But when you see him, don't expect Moses or Isaiah or Herzl look-alikes.

Uri's home is filled with religious books, mostly the Talmud and its related commentaries and codes, and Biblical commentaries. Torah is critical in his life. He teaches religious subjects and supervises Judaica courses in one of Jerusalem's schools. That's what he does for a living. What he *does*, though, is touch the lives of thousands of people throughout Israel — daily. For his real work he gets no salary. He gets other things, of course: joy, satisfaction, a sense of wellbeing, meaning, and all those other exquisite Intangibles of Life.

I am drawing another blank....I can't remember exactly how it all got started. You can find out the origins of Yad Sarah in detail from Uri himself. It might have been an offspring of some other Tzedakah work he and his family were doing; it might have been a simple-revelation-leading-to-a-specific-act. I just don't remember.

But the fact is, about a dozen years ago Uri obtained Yad Sarah's first medical equipment and set up a lending station in his home. It must have hit a sensitive nerve in Israel, because it grew and grew at such a pace, no one even 5 years ago would have thought it would be this big today...let alone in the very beginning. Medical care is good in Israeli hospitals, but there was so much more to the picture of the physical and psychological welfare of the people that needed to be covered. Yad Sarah filled that gap and has ultimately saved thousands of lives, prevented thousands of hospital admissions, eased thousands upon thousands of days of home care, made life easier, more manageable and pleasant for too many people to keep track of with a good-sized computer.

There is no question that the very nature of this Mitzvah work has drawn in many volunteers. But it is equally clear that Uri's personality is the major force in Yad Sarah's growth and development. By dint of who he is as a person, Uri has set the tone of the project: gentle, decent, caring, all human contact to be managed in a manner that preserves everyone's dignity...in short, as a Mensch.

Now Uri is quite normal. He can be playful and joking, and he enjoys a good picnic out in the hills with his people (with songs thrown in as the food sizzles on the grill) as much as the next person. But he can also be angelic. By that I mean someone who exudes Menschlichkeit in all his words and actions. He has a certain innocence about him, but he is not a sucker to be trampled on by insensitive bureaucracies or individuals within those bureaucracies. He has a radiance, a certain something in his bearing that sets you at ease and immediately makes you realize you are sitting with or standing with or working with a fine, fine person. And that, sitting or standing or working with Uri, you sense that — whatever your own deficiencies or shortcomings — you want to be like him in some way, to be like him and to do things as he does them. And that sitting or standing or working with Uri, you promise yourself that you *will* indeed attempt to do just that, find more of the Uri in you.

What it comes down to is this: *he does this because this is what people do for each other. Plain and simple.* These *are* Mitzvahs, after all. Whether or not he believes that absolutely every single human being on God's earth can live this way, I can't say, but I know he knows there are more and more Mitzvah people out there than anyone can imagine. And he and Yad Sarah are helping many people discover these Mitzvah urgings within themselves. People who would have never seen themselves doing such High Mitzvahs are doing them everywhere.

Let me illustrate. When my summer is over, one of my friends usually takes me to the airport. I like to take the El Al late night flight which gets me back to Kennedy around 5:00 or 6:00 a.m. so I can be back in Washington early in the day. The plane leaves Tel Aviv around midnight or 1:00 a.m. Last summer or the summer before last, my other friends were tied up, so I called Uri. Of course he would take me, though I still wonder where one of the busiest and most important Mitzvah people around finds time to drive people to the airport in the middle of the night. Beyond that, I knew that there would be no need to be embarrassed if I asked him to take me. It would be his pleasure.

Let me illustrate again how attractive Uri's personality is in this World of Mitzvahs and how he draws people into Yad Sarah's work. I have told this story in a previous book, but it bears re-telling. Next door to the building that houses Yad Sarah's national office is the organization's Jerusalem headquarters. It looks very much like an old railroad car from Rakevet Yisrael, Israel Railroads. In fact, it *is* an old railroad car from Rakevet Yisrael, and it is a good couple of miles from the end of the Jerusalem railroad tracks.

This is how it wound up on the empty lot next to the national office:

One day, Uri was concerned that they needed more space. He needed something easy to set up that could accommodate the Jerusalem office. He first considered "containers", those mammoth steel boxes used for shipping, but rejected the idea. (No windows? Too drab? No flair?) Then he thought of a railroad car. So he called Rakevet Yisrael and asked if they had any spare railroad cars. Indeed they did, the Rakevet Yisrael man said. Uri then asked if he could have one of them, and the man said that indeed he could. So, after fixing it up in Haifa where it had been sitting on some siding, it was brought down to Jerusalem. A number of streets were closed in the middle of the night. A mammoth-crane owner (private or army I don't recall) was called to lend a hand (or claw) to Yad Sarah with some of his Magic, Mammoth Cranes, and the railroad car was shlepped to HaNevi'im Street. That seems simple enough, and typical of the way The Grandest Mitzvah Bandwagon in Israel works. (Yad Sarah is the largest volunteer organization in the country.)

This tone-of-operation that Uri has established and that Yad Sarah projects lends support to one of my particular contentions: the same sum-total of Mitzvah work accomplished — even more — can be accomplished if it is supervised and run in a Menschlich fashion...the same sum-total that might have been accomplished by other means. In the world of Mitzvah work there are apparently a wide variety of Mitzvah administrators: executive-types who may or may not be particularly Menschlich but who are very good at administering Mitzvah projects; executive-types who may or may not be particularly Menschlich who could just as well be administering an insurance company or bank or real estate office; Uri-like individuals who may or may not be particularly skilled administrators, and all shadings in between. Ideally a project would want all the best elements in its director: Menschlich, committed to the Mitzvah work, and a good administrator. The problem arises when you can't find all three qualities in one person. Do you select the Mensch, even at the cost of possibly sloppy administration, or do you pick the super-administrator, even though he or she does not personify the human qualities the Mitzvah work represents? Even if Uri were the worst administrator in the world (which he is not), Yad Sarah proves my point. In the crude language of the bottom line — producing the necessary end results of reaching people — the Mensch is the appropriate administrator-of-choice.

I sense that bad choices are being made by boards of directors in many areas of Mitzvah work. Sometimes there is a bitter or sour taste left in the mouths of people who watch the bad choices in action. They wonder how there can be such a disparity between the uplifting goals of the organization and the unpleasant nature of the director. And some people — volunteers, second-level professionals, contributors — leave the Mitzvah organization for that reason...which, in turn, damages the Bottom Line.

Enough said.

URI AND YAD SARAH IN ACTION

I want to zero in on one particular type of medical equipment Yad Sarah lends for free. (Actually I lied: you have to leave a nominal deposit, which is returned when you bring the equipment back.) The device is called a respiration or apnea monitor. It is a very small piece of equipment weighing less than 2 pounds, and it is computerized. A thin, insulated wire descends from the device and is taped to a baby. What it does is simple: if the baby stops breathing, very loud alarms go off and lights begin to flash. The baby wakes up by itself and begins breathing normally again, or a family member comes running in to survey the situation. It is

Uri Lupoliansky displays one of the many awards received by the
Yad Sarah organization.

a major weapon in the fight against crib death (or Sudden Infant Death as it is also
known). But it costs Yad Sarah close to $1,000 each.

According to Dr. Kalman Mann, former director of Hadassah Hospital in
Jerusalem, eminent physician, and chairman of Yad Sarah's board of directors, the
statistics worldwide would suggest the possibility of 150 crib deaths a year in Israel.

So this is a well-defined problem, a life-and-death situation with a decent
probability of real and calculable results. The greater and more real-and-immediate
problem is providing monitors for people who cannot afford to buy them. What do
they do if the doctors have discovered a tendency in the infant to stop breathing?
The answer: Yad Sarah. Loaned out free.

Here is a letter Yad Sarah received in 1987 from one couple that had availed
themselves of Yad Sarah's services:

Dear Yad Sarah,

*In January of this year we discovered that our son Noam, then eight
weeks old was experiencing interruptions in his breathing during
sleep.*

For nights we took turns staying up to make sure that his breath does return as we were both aware that stoppages at this age could be and are sometimes fatal.

At a later point in time our family doctor who was becoming aware of the effects of the lack of sleep on ourselves and our family, suggested we turn to Yad Sarah for a respiration monitor.

On January 10 we went to Yad Sarah and were issued the monitor right away and with astoundingly little red-tape. The staff was very pleasant to deal with and the explanation as to the use of the device was full and comforting.

Having the respiration monitor at home has made it possible for us to almost return to our normal routines. At first it used to go off many times each night but with time these incidents lessened. We now find that we get enough sleep so that we can again give both our children the kind of parenting they deserve and carry out our respective tasks properly.

Noam underwent an exhaustive battery of tests in which nothing was found wrong and the interruptions in his breathing now fall within normal range. The consensus among the doctors who treated him is that he stay monitored during his sleep for another four weeks as a matter of safety.

We both wish to express our thanks to Yad Sarah and its staff for making their help so readily available at such time as it was most needed.

Sincerely yours,

Uri had also told me another story of a woman who had lost one child to crib death, and with the birth of a second child, she would *never* leave the baby...even taking it into the bathroom with her. When she obtained a monitor from Yad Sarah, her life returned to normal.

And there was another one, where a double round of Yad Sarah's intervention was needed: the woman had developed diabetes during her pregnancy. It was serious and the doctors wanted her to stay in the hospital for the duration of the pregnancy. She obtained a glucometer from Yad Sarah, went home, took her own blood sugar counts and called in the results as frequently as the doctors wanted...and led a much more normal life during those difficult months. Then the baby was born, and the doctors discovered a mysterious tendency to stop breathing. The woman got a respiration monitor from Yad Sarah, and life once again returned to normal.

Imagine the masses of equipment on loan: all those wheelchairs, hospital beds, crutches, Canadian crutches, walkers, air mattresses, hearing aids, suction pumps, glucometers, patient lifts, Neurogard pain-relieving devices, breast pumps, humidifiers, and so many other kinds of simple and complex items, all circulated by an incredibly large lending operation. The mind would be hard pressed to conceive of how many people on any given day are benefiting from the Mitzvah labors of the Yad Sarah people and their inspiration, Uri.

Add this: a mobile lending station that reaches the out-of-the-way parts of Israel, an emergency alarm system in Jerusalem (by merely pressing a button, a central computer locates the person in need of assistance), a laundry service for individuals who have become incontinent, a mobile electric wheelchair repair unit that goes to people's homes to fix even the most complicated mechanized wheelchairs, and a repair shop and an equipment manufacturing establishment, often employing elderly, retired individuals. *And* a model apartment set up with the latest devices, tools, and equipment to demonstrate what is available for people with disabilities.

Imagine all that with (as of April 1, 1988) 3,270 volunteers and only 19 1/3 salaried people! That's about 3/5 of one paid employee per 100 volunteers.

How do they do it?

Ask Uri.

Ask anyone who works for Yad Sarah.

There's no real secret.

IN SUM

There is something sacred about the configuration and mood of Yad Sarah. I am sure that along the way there have been some unpleasant incidents when people have come to borrow equipment. But how many of these incidents can be counted in a dozen years and hundreds of thousands of moments-of-encounter? Too few to mention.

The all-pervading character of Yad Sarah remains Menschlich, and, as I have said, sacred. There is holy work taking place in its lending stations throughout Israel. For all the enormous sum of human pain encountered, it is neither a discouraging nor a depressing atmosphere. The Spirit of Mitzvahs and the Joy of Mitzvahs prevails and is very infectious.

Jews and non-Jews work for Yad Sarah. And Jews and non-Jews have full lending rights to the equipment. It is a sphere of immunity from religious tensions between Jews and non-Jews.

Jews of every kind work for Yad Sarah. Religious Jews and non-religious Jews and people in between; left-leaning and right-leaning and centrists; rich, poor, university professor and common laborer alike. It is a protected space from Jewish religious and non-religious tensions, a haven and a refuge for those who want to forget their differences and just simply concentrate on the work at hand, namely getting vital medical equipment and adjunct services into the lives of people who need the equipment and services, at no cost and no loss of dignity. Yad Sarah personifies Shalom, Peace, as Uri Lupoliansky personifies Shalom, Peace.

Uri and Uri's Yad Sarah have won many awards in Israel. They seem to be forever winning prizes. One of them, presented by the Israeli Government, is most significant in this context. It is an award for Achdut Am Yisrael — Unifying the Jewish People. Jewish tradition, so much a part of Uri's life, teaches that Mitzvahs were given to people to tie them together. Yad Sarah is the realization of that ancient text in our own day.

Uri Lupoliansky, c/o Yad Sarah, 43 HaNevi' im St., Jerusalem, 244-047.

REFLECTIONS VI

There is such a startling and mysterious variety of people I wish to describe. They look like everybody-you-ever-saw or nobody or nobody-in-particular, and they are short and tall and somewhere in between, and stocky and thin and of average weight, bearded and otherwise, physically attractive, plain looking, and even less-than-plain, speaking inordinately rapidly and, on the other side of the scale, so slowly you urge on every next word from them.

So many people and so many kinds of people. It is difficult to discern patterns.

So, too, their Mitzvah projects....They flourish in such a startling and equally mysterious variety of ways. There are projects to repair cleft palates for free and others designed to bring gloves to the freezing hands of homeless people, feeding programs, programs to teach people the alphabet or Alef-Bet or Alpha-Beta, refugee projects, eyeglass projects and seeing-eye dog projects and hearing aid projects and hearing dog-projects and projects to lend dishes at no charge for weddings (and bands, photographers, halls, and food).

So many projects and so many kinds of Mitzvah projects. It is difficult to find patterns.

Age seems to be no determining factor. One person, Trevor Ferrell, began at age 11, and others I know of started earlier on in life. There are quite a number who get a late awakening; they are well into their 50's and beyond. No, age can't be a determining factor.

Some create the Mitzvah work on their own...as it were, out of the blue, while others have it thrust upon them from the outside due to war or economics or changing neighborhoods or a family circumstance or any one of a number of other factors. Something arises that triggers a reaction; they react in Mitzvah fashion, and their lives change, radically, gradually, or somewhere in between. I have seen neither the "out of the blue" nor the "outside circumstance" origins predominate. Some people even seem to just stumble on a Mitzvah while they are doing nothing in particular; nothing catastrophic has happened to move them to action — they are just in the right place at the right time.

Some of the heroes described here seem to have had major revelations, and others only gradually moved into their present work. For the ones who had revelations, the stimulus needn't have been necessarily earthshaking. It could have been the most minor of details or date or happenings, though this last point is particularly thrilling to watch as it takes shape: an insight, ever so simple, takes hold of the person — sometimes to the point of obsession. An observer blessed with hindsight might be skeptical seeing the vast end results that supposedly sprang from such an ostensibly minor idea. Is it possible that so much could come of such an obvious and elementary beginning? Well, obvious now....Beforehand it wasn't so obvious.

In other realms of human experience this "Simple Revelation Factor" has certainly been evident. In medicine, consider Ignaz Semmelweis a hundred years ago, insisting that doctors wash their hands between autopsies and delivering babies or performing gynecological examinations. Such a simple thing — washing the hands. How many millions of lives have been saved as a result? How few people today even know of puerperal ("childbed") fever, the scourge that killed mothers of newborns in plague proportions a little more than a century ago? Think of mold in a dish that somehow became penicillin once Sir Alexander Fleming made the connection.

The same has been true in literature: a sound, an image, a thing of apparently little consequence becomes the basis of a poem or play or novel, a piece of literature that will live for centuries, millenia. Think of Marcel Proust's little pastry, one from his long-ago childhood and the long, rolling, marvellous passages that came from it in Remembrance of Things Past. *And though I have little background in music, I would imagine there are symphonies and concertos that sprang from the conjunction of two or three notes in some composer's head on a not-particularly-inspiring or gorgeous day. And masterpieces of painting. Certainly art historians can tell us which ones fired a certain painter's imagination because of things we non-painters might just pass by: the particular shape of a bridge, an off color on some lawn, the motion of a boxer falling to the mat of some ring in an overcrowded gym reeking of sweat.*

Some people are asleep or drowsing or just rising from sleep when the Mitzvah idea is set in motion in their minds. For sure, all levels of the mind have come into play for different Mitzvah heroes...the unconscious, the subconscious, the conscious mind. There are hazy states of activity that psychologists and psychiatrists continue to explore to try to understand these phenomena, but, empirically — just studying the Mitzvah heroes and the results of their Mitzvah acts — we know it is true: some start projects which have their origins in the machinations *of one level of the mind, some on some other level, and still others in combination. Some Mitzvah heroes were totally aware of what was happening from the outset, and others still could not see the magnificence of it all until they were in the very thick of the action.*

Arthur Koestler explored much of the theory of artistic and scientific creativity in his book, The Act of Creation. *But no one that I know of has done as thorough and systematic a study of the origins of great Mitzvah acts. It would be most worthwhile. I would now offer somewhat haphazardly one or two theories, partially based on Koestler's explorations of creativity in other areas of human experience:*

What is clear is that one's previous training and experiences in life can *provide more or less fertile ground for Mitzvah work. Ideally, Mitzvahs are central for the Jewish people; the idea of Mitzvahs suffuses the holy books, and Mitzvahs are "in the air" in the community. Ideally, that is. If Mitzvahs were studied and actualized more in the educational system, the foundation would be laid for greater and greater results. I am certain this is true for other religious traditions. Many of the people I describe got their "start" from religious insights: their Jewish or Catholic or Protestant teachings expect this kind of life of kindness and giving-to-others from their adherents. But some of the Mitzvah heroes come from outside of a religious setting. Some heroes may come from a strong moral or ethical or humanitarian frame of reference or some other similar tradition. And most mysterious of all — there are some Mitzvah heroes, who, as it were, "come from out of nowhere", with no obvious link in their pasts that would lead their students and apprentices to understand just how they came to be doing what they are doing: saving lives, restoring dignity, doing wonders.*

What the Mitzvah heroes all have in common is that they are saving lives and alleviating suffering and rebuilding broken human beings and raising others to more exalted heights of humanity, though their approaches might be totally different. Some do it because of Tzedek and Tzedakah — Justice and Righteousness, The Right Thing: some do it because of Christian love, and some others out of simple common decency. But I want to make it clear: it is the end results which remain my main interest. The origins and even Ultimate Origins of Mitzvah work are only an added feature of my involvement. The theoretical must always remain, at least in my mind, of relatively secondary importance to the Mitzvah acts themselves.

I would make something clear at this point. As a Jew, I am not equating Mitzvah work with Judaism. There is so much more to the religion of my ancestors than just performing these acts of Justice and Righteousness. The survival and thriving of the State of Israel, Torah study, the rituals, to name a few, take their appropriate places in my thinking. But the centrality of Tzedakah and Tzedek action is a sine qua non, *without which Judaism is drained of its vigor.*

There is one other point I would add to someone's future systematic study of Mitzvah Heroes and Their Acts: it appears to me that the extent, grandeur, and intensity of the Mitzvah Hero's work in no way depends *on the Hero's IQ. For some reason, there is no* necessary *connection between the two, between intellectual capabilities and Mitzvah capabilities. At least that has been my experience. I would not go so far as to say that exceptionally bright people are less apt to be Mitzvah heroes, but I would not shy away from saying that many intellectuals fail to come through in this all-important area of human existence. There are even a few who, in fact, sometimes wallow in their own brightness and do not partake of the majesty of Mitzvah work, and some smaller numbers who use their exceptional brain power for destructive acts rather than Mitzvahs. It is a bitter conclusion to reach, and sad. It hurts to record this after a dozen years of thinking about it and watching people in action. On the other end of the scale, it would be unfair to say that all people of what is all-too-commonly (and detrimentally) referred to as "average" or "below average" intelligence have a greater tendency to Mitzvah work. That simply is not true. But not having a dazzling intelligence quotient and aca-*

demic record in no way affects a human being's ability to triumph in the World of Mitzvahs.

As a Jewish educator, that last paragraph means to me that, if, on the most basic-of-basic levels we would like to live in a better, more decent world, our efforts must be put primarily on Mitzvahs and Mitzvah heroes and leave the intellectual side of things in a lesser position in the curriculum. Facts, figures, and scholarship should not be ignored, but they should never supersede the quest for creating a world that is Just and Righteous and Fair, pleasant, decent and peaceful.

Let us begin the New Era with more Mitzvah Heroes and a multitude of Mitzvah acts.

HEROES OF THE VALLEY

I am so confused about the government's policy on Central American refugees that I don't know whether or not I should be using these heroes' real names. It is difficult to determine if what they are doing is legal, illegal, or a combination of both. If I identify them, it may jeopardize their work and wellbeing. So to play it safe, I will be circumspect and alter the heroes' identities. Only the members of my own group are mentioned by their real names.

FATHER MIKE

Father Mike is young; he's Irish by descent, and *very* lively. He ministers to thousands of people: legal residents and citizens, illegals, and those in the process of applying for some form of safe status. The day my friends and I met him he was in the middle of preparing for his fifth or sixth week-end Mass, besides sharing with another priest the ceremony of anointing the sick. For that event, which I had never seen before, I sat in the back of the church and watched compassion flow from Father Mike's fingertips as he recited the appropriate words to each person, put a sign on their foreheads, then hugged and kissed each one. He was in his white robes now, ever so different than when I first saw him in jeans and a casual monogrammed T-shirt back at the rectory.

Those two images together gave me the most complete picture of Father Mike: the jeans-and-T-shirted man and the robed pastor. When we entered his home somewhere deep in the Rio Grande Valley —nearly 2,000 miles from his birthplace in Boston — the TV was blasting away with a baseball game. In his everyday clothes he looks like an ordinary Red Sox fan. And yet, a few minutes later, he would be in the church, a pastor...Padre Mike as his people call him. "Pastor" means "shepherd" in Latin, and here in the church he was a shepherd as the Bible meant a shepherd to be. There was a sense of holiness pervading his presence — in his robes and even in his jeans and T-shirt.

It made no difference how Father Mike looked on the outside; you could feel the sanctity however he was dressed, so powerful is his passion for Justice and Dignity. He emanates an aura of goodness.

What is it about Father Mike that draws us all to him? First, there is his extraordinary kindness, a tireless kindness, a sincere-to-the-bones kindness. Father Mike extends himself to his flock to an extraordinary degree through long, very hot and very humid days and nights. As he takes us around the *colonias* (the poverty neighborhoods), the houses where poverty reeks differently than in the ghettoes of the North and Northeast, but reeks no less for it's Latin American-Texas accent — we have the opportunity to exchange religious thoughts. (What the Jews would call words of Torah.) Many aspects of our theology merge, his of the Catholic Church, ours from our Jewish training: all people are created in the Image of God, and because of that Divine Image, human beings are entitled to a certain human response

from all of us. That is how Father Mike defines himself. You can see it in the way
he talks and the way he moves his powerfully-built body. He physically resembles
a tough sailor or wrestler or boxer, and this physical power and energy could just
as well be used to tear someone's face away in the ring or in some back alley. But
this is Father Mike, and he uses his power and energy for Mitzvah work.

Then there is Father Mike's ability to share the pain of the people. He's
from the Northeast, of Irish ancestry, and yet the Mexicans, the Guatemalans, the
Hondurans and Salvadorans and Nicaraguans are his congregation, his brothers
and sisters....Even more, they are a part of his body, part of his blood through a
common lineage stretching all the way back to Adam and Eve. His heart breaks for
the suffering of his people, and his brokenheartedness is authentic and vast. It is
part of what makes him who he is. Many of his flock live in desperate fear of de-
portation — for some an almost-certain death. Others would face suffering of
unimaginable proportions. The fear and suffering are not remote or theoretical for
Father Mike. It is *his* fear, *he* is unable to sleep at night, it terrorizes *him* in a most
personal way. For Father Mike there is no "I" and "they"; their terror is his own.

And his anger, prophetic, explosive, righteous. Prophetic and explosive,
for sure. If you could imagine Isaiah or Jeremiah dressed in jeans and a T-shirt,
you would know the prophet himself. Touch the tender part of his soul with the
needle of cruelty and exploitation and he explodes in pain, battering his listeners
with the complaints of the sufferers, the agonies of their being trampled upon with
no possible justification. "Justification", "righteous anger" — we are back at the
word "Tzedek" in Hebrew, "Justice", "The Right Thing", "setting aright the ugly
wrongs visited upon God's creations." If a Righteous Person, a Tzaddik, is one
who takes upon himself the injustices and imbalances of senseless cruelties in this
world, leaving behind a dazzling light wherever he steps, then Father Mike is a
Tzaddik. He may primarily see his work in the Rio Grande Valley as an act of
Christian love, but that does not preclude the element of Tzedek. His giving-of-
himself is the personification of Justice in a part-of-the-world-gone-crazy.

And Father Mike's enthusiasm. That word comes from the root "Theos",
"God". He is filled with God; he spends hours in prayer and leading others in
prayer. You do not have to be a believer in his type of religion. You don't even
have to believe that religion is worth anything at all to see and feel Father Mike's
whole being filled with God's presence.

This is the Rio Grande Valley (or, as the people living there call it, just "The
Valley") where people cross the river night or day to find refuge and relief. Some
of the people are Mexicans who are desperate to earn a wage that will sustain themselves and their families. Some are Nicaraguans. By American law and by the actions of the Immigration and Naturalization Service they are defined as political
refugees and have a relatively easy time obtaining transit passes to other places in
the States. They also experience a similarly relatively smooth process to receive
asylum. Others who come over the Rio Grande are from Honduras, Guatemala,

and El Salvador, and they are The Ones Who Hide; they are The Hunted. The government defines them as "economic refugees", not "officially" in imminent danger of being murdered or tortured and, therefore, unentitled to such an easy process of ingathering. These latter three classes of individuals need protection, help in processing their papers, legal defense, a place to sleep and eat and, most of all, to be treated with dignity.

Many of the Central American refugees have been robbed of everything they own by the *coyotes*, the ones who, for a price, bring them over the border.

And some of them have been raped by the *coyotes*.

And some of them have been beaten.

And some, whom we do not see, (and only hear about through the network) have been murdered with near-freedom in sight.

And none of them can just drive or ride or walk into the Greater United States once they are over the border. Up the main highways a few miles or 50 miles or 100 miles are checkpoints, and every car passing through is stopped, and if you are illegal, you are detained and the process begins to send you back — particularly for the Salvadorans, Hondurans, and Guatelmalans.

These are some of Father Mike's people. That is their world in Texas, in The Valley, in 1988.

I like his tattoos. I don't know where and when he got them, but they are on his arms and they add a certain flair to his presence. Padre Mike is about 37 or 38 years old, younger than I am, and, as often happens, I wonder what I was doing at his age five or six years ago that might compare in some way to his life's work. I kept losing something in the translation...when he was speaking English. His Boston accent is so thick, and he speaks with such speed and passion when he is worked up over something, I couldn't always follow. But what came through so clearly was that he is so very, very real.

His life is useful.

He is serving God as he feels he should.

He is at home with himself, and for all the pain and suffering he sees daily, he is not a sad or depressed person. His is a life of joy, of great meaning to himself and those who meet him and are blessed by his presence.

When Father Mike was ordained, the Church wanted to place him on Cape Cod. He fought it. He knew he would waste away up there. Even then, a priest fresh out of training, he knew his place was with The People.

From Father Mike's standpoint: We were a group of eight Jews coming down to see and take part ever-so-briefly in the life of the refugees. One of the group, Laurie Lemel, from Madison, Wisconsin, had spent a few years down here. She had gotten her Rabbi, Charles Feinberg, involved, and, with him, made arrangements to bring Rabbis and other Jews to see what the refugee situation was all about. Rabbi Feinberg had been down once before this trip. He is a friend of mine and tried to get me to go a year ago. He knew I must go, and though I missed the first trip, I finally got there this time, April, 1988.

Eight of us would be there in all. Some arrived late, but for those of us who got there early enough on Sunday, we would eat dinner with Father Mike. A small group of other people who had been working on behalf of the refugees for varying lengths of time— a nun, a paralegal, residents of The Valley — would also join us for the meal.

Three of us got there in the afternoon, and in minutes his home was our home.

We had a few minutes with Padre Mike, and then he was off to anoint the sick. Then dinner, but Padre Mike was gone for most of it, busy with his people. Finally, towards the end of the meal, he appeared, and took us on a tour of the *Colonias.* The tour ended, we went back to Father Mike's house (which is not his house, but the Church's) and, standing by the car outside, we hugged and said good-bye.

Now I am home, nine days later, sitting in front of what feels like a dumb machine, a Macintosh word processor, a tool, a piece of machinery one level removed from reality, filled with microchips and keys and the latest electronic trickery, and I am very lonely. I wonder why I am here and not there. I knew that when we drove away from Father Mike and the World of Father Mike, I knew that eight days later, a day later, ten minutes later, I would be lonely, perhaps even a little frightened that my world was not the real world. I am lonely because I need Father Mike, his teachings, his righteous anger, his straightforward and simple love, just one more hug, perhaps every morning and every night, at the beginning and end of a long day of Mitzvah-work.

Just one more hug, maybe two, every day from Father Mike.

INTERLUDE

I don't believe in fate. Even though there is a fine Yiddish word — *Bashert* — that I have heard over and over again among the Jews, I don't think that things work out so clearly in life that you could say definitively that they are "fated" to turn out in a particular way.

I also have some doubts about high-sounding words and concepts like "eschatological" and "apocalyptic", all those events relating to the "End of Days". There are supposed to be enormous upheavals in the world, a gargantuan change in the nature of life before Messianic Times set in. I recall another august-sounding term, a Latin phrase — *"sub specie aeternitatis"* — "under the eyes of Eternity", meaning, I would imagine, seeing events in the broadest sense of things, in their grandest meanings.

Nevertheless, sometime during this trip to The Valley, I wondered again and again why it was I took four years of Spanish in highschool some 30 years ago. At best I have used it on rare occasions over the last three decades. Once or twice I have taken up some poetry by Pablo Neruda, the Chilean Nobel Prize Winner, or spoken a few words here and there to someone whose native tongue was Spanish, but that's all.

Then, all of a sudden, I find myself on the Texas-Mexican border, speaking haltingly, but understanding 60-70% of the conversations of the refugees and their hosts. I listen to Suffering on the Grand Scale, and even though we have translators, it is important that I try to hear the stories directly from the refugees themselves. I have to hear it in Spanish, so nothing will be lost.

I still don't believe in the high-sounding words, but I am stunned. It is something to consider, to wonder about — that whim in the late 1950's to pick Spanish rather than French or some other language. Why should it be, and why should I have ever considered that thirty years down the road I would be looking in the eyes of mothers who walked or rode on beat-up buses hundreds of miles from El Salvador and Guatemala and other Central American countries, brought over the border by savage *coyotes* to tell me their stories?

BROTHER JUAN

For our Jewish group, many stretches of the Rio Grande seemed like the Jordan River — smaller than expected. Some parts of it are dangerous, deep, with swift currents, but the crossing points seem very modest, and it is hardly as romantic as the old Western movies and Country Western songs would have us believe.

We stood at one well-known place where Central American refugees and Mexican day-workers and migrants (some of this story concerns Mexicans, also) cross over into America. The water was shallow enough for people to wade through with their clothes and other possessions held over their heads. The city of Matamoros was across the Rio Grande on the Mexican side; freedom was over here.

Our guide for the morning was Juan, an American of Mexican ancestry and a near-mythological figure to those who know him. He spoke in Spanish. He is a Mennonite, with a big kibbutznik-like mustache, and I kept noticing that one of his shoes seemed to have more substantial soles than the other one. Since I had ridden out to this place in a different car than Juan's, I hadn't noticed till he was started walking back to his car that he was disabled. He had been injured in a work-related accident, and the limp was his legacy.

As we talked and took pictures, three young people who had just crossed The River passed behind us on the path. We looked away and let them pass, surprized that it all happened so simply in the middle of the morning. The setting was complete. We had not seen them cross — they must have been downstream a bit — but they were indeed newly-arrived, just a few minutes ago, and they were on their way.

Brother Juan spoke softly, but with great passion. This Brother Juan says he just does what he has to do. And what he does is simple: when people cross over The River, many of them seek out a local church. The word of new arrivals is passed around the network, and Juan and his people, and more people like him all over The Valley, take care of them, feed them, clothe them, give them shelter, begin the process of paperwork and forms, treat them with the human touch they might not have known for a long time. Day in and day out. Tirelessly.

I would say Brother Juan is about my age, maybe a few years older, and I don't remember how long he has been doing this holy work. But it is clear that he will not retire to a "normal" life until everyone who comes to his home and to his friends and to his church (he is only a layperson, not a clergyman) for a roof and a meal and an extended hand — until every single one of them is provided with what he or she needs.

Our group wanted to know how and why Brother Juan became involved in this Mitzvah-work. One incident came to Juan's mind, a story from his childhood. He was seven or eight or nine years old and out by the Rio Grande one day when he saw someone cross The River. The "illegal" was spotted by a member of the Border Patrol in his jeep. The refugee hid in the tall grass. (We could see the grass all around us.) The patrolman lost sight of him but rode his jeep back and forth and back and forth again through the grass trying to ferret him out. Finally the patrolman left, unable to find the man. Juan recalls how much the man in hiding seemed like a trapped animal and the patrolman a hunter. Now, in 1988, Brother Juan stands at a similar spot, telling us about the incident — it may be the hundredth or thousandth time he's told the story. But the scene still wells up inside of him with great surges of passion and sympathy. We are deeply moved, and a little uncomfortable that we might have pried too much, though Juan does not give us that feeling at all.

Brother Juan also seems somewhat prophet-like, but he is much more restrained. He recites the tale anew, not mechanically, but with quiet, eloquent sadness, a story he must tell again and again until the world changes. That is what makes him like a prophet. He won't ever become anyone else than himself — a human-being-who-is-a-haven for the hunted. And since he won't change who he is, the world must become a place where there are no more human beings hunted down like animals. Until then, he will recite the same story again and again and other stories just like it, until the world gets it right.

It is eight days later. I am back in my safe apartment without a doorman (we don't need one; it's a good neighborhood), on the seventh floor, typing away. As with Father Mike, I miss Brother Juan; I am lonely for his kind face, his naturalness, his stories-as-intense-as-Elie-Wiesel's, his lack of anything resembling the slick or the wily. He is, like Father Mike, *very* real: his devotion to the people who come to his door befits him; he is comfortable with his mission; he is at home in this hot, humid place, this border where people come for safety and sanctuary, and there is no doubt in his soul that this is where God wants him to be for as long as it takes to complete his holy task.

Juan — like so many others — would hardly consider himself a hero. But he *is* a hero. He is neither a myth nor "near-mythological", as I wrote above.

If "hero" means "human-as-human-can-be", he is most assuredly a hero, flesh and blood, with a touch of the angelic.

HOSTS AND HOSPITALITY

We were to have lunch with a young couple who, through their church, help to organize the people of the *colonias*, those devastatingly poor neighborhoods on the fringes of The Valley's cities and towns. They were going to talk with us and take us around, showing us the *colonias* and their church where people would be helping refugees fill out forms for the INS, others giving medical assistance... people giving all kinds of help, encouragement, and hope.

Our hosts had misunderstood the plans, and since early morning had been preparing a meal for us at their house. Since we were the first group of Jews to go down to The Valley as a group, they most certainly did not know about our rules of keeping Kosher, and, as we suspected when we got their home, the meal consisted of a variety of foods that were outside the realm of our religious practice.

That was all right, though. They understood. We went to a restaurant and no offense was taken.

They humbly told us the story of their work, their caring, their devotion, the simplicity of that devotion — topics we had come to recognize over and over again. And though we heard similar stories a number of times, we were always moved, always astounded at the depth and extent of the compassion of the people. There were tales or success and failure, variations on a theme, but always the same theme: people giving without ulterior motives to others, fully, warmly. As Leviticus 19:18 would have it, "Love thy neighbor as thyself".

What began to seep in, though, was that we were the first group of Jews that had come down to see the situation first hand. Individuals had come through, and there were some Jewish people who were working in The Valley...lawyers, paralegals, volunteers. But as a *group*, the four Rabbis and the four others were a most unusual set of people to come into their homes. It was something to think about as we continued our rounds of visits.

THE UNITED FARM WORKERS LOCAL

Everyone in our group knew about the grape boycott from twenty years ago. When Cesar Chavez organized the migrant workers, many, if not all, of us joined his efforts to empower the workers and to win their contracts...and to make real gains for some degree of better treatment for the people who wander from place to place to pick the fruits and vegetables that are on our dining room tables.

And still we were shocked. From the moment we began to listen to the United Farm Workers members who spoke to us, we were appalled.

We were astounded to learn that many of the Federal labor laws specifically exclude farm workers, though there have been a few changes.

We were shocked to learn that some of the issues for the UFW included water to drink out in the fields, bathroom facilities, a place to wash one's hands after taking care of one's personal needs. These seemed so basic and so obvious, and yet they must be fought for.

We were shocked (or at least I was — some of the others had more background) to hear that so much of the cropland is owned by corporations — insurance companies and other multi-layered firms that don't even sound like they would include tomatoes and avocados and onions in their portfolios.

We were shocked that in union elections there are threats and stolen ballot boxes and Old-Wild-West-style violence...even shootings. We were disgusted.

We were shocked at the sheer poverty of the people, the number of accidents that wreak havoc on the lives and health of the laborers, the enormous distances the migrants travel around the country to eke out a bare-minimum living.

But most of all, we were horrified by the lethal hazards of pesticides. One of the UFW workers (my age, a little younger perhaps) told us that years ago, when she used to work in the fields and the cropduster planes would approach, the workers were told just to lie down in the fields until the spraying was finished. *They were covered with the chemicals, soaked.*

And this woman told us that when she was breast-feeding her child a few years ago, they still found DDT in her milk...fifteen years after she had been sprayed.

DDT is now banned, but other toxic chemicals are being used And even though states like Texas and California now have stringent pesticide laws, they still spray with the same disregard for human life and welfare as they did years ago, and there are at least five pesticides that still carry all the dangers one would suspect: death, cancer, children born deformed, children developing leukemia and other fatal diseases, cutting short their lives, thousands of workers living with The Long Wait, the examinations at the doctor's office or clinic, waiting for the bad news.

Yesterday I saw the UFW videotape of the present grape boycott. It's called "The Wrath of Grapes", and it's all there: the weeping mother and father of a child with no arms and legs: the seven-year-old child with leukemia; the company thug lifting a metal chair over a union worker at the UFW election, swinging it high over his head, bringing it down on the worker; the mother of the young worker who died so quickly in a recently-sprayed field; the UFW doctor explaining how dangerous-toxic-lethal the pesticides are; how some residue remains on the grapes and can't be washed off; how California refuses to enforce the law; how the companies claim they can't hang up warning signs in recently-sprayed fields because "they can't afford it"; how neighborhoods and *schools* near fields are sprayed. It's all there in the video. (If you want a copy of the videotape, write United Farm

Workers-Texas Project, POB 188, San Juan, Texas, 78589. A contribution —
$18, $25 — would be appropriate.)

It *is* horrible. Perhaps it is too much to take in at once, all that we learned at
the meeting at the UFW...and then the video.

I would suggest concentrating instead on just one story: a young woman
lying, face to the ground, stretched out in the fields, as the plane buzzes overhead,
spraying its deadly chemicals.

THE REFUGE THAT IS LIKE A KIBBUTZ

Dinner one night was at a 40-acre refuge somewhere in The Valley. Most
of the people there are Salvadorans and the place is run by a committee, very much
like a Kibbutz. The refuge is a gift from an immigration lawyer, and it is a place for
people waiting for some degree of more stable legal status to get settled...and to do
some good work. There are fields and crops, some horses and cows, and most of
all, there is a place to live that is safe, pleasant, and dignified.

Dinner was carefully arranged, and the refugees worked hard to serve us
vegetables and fish according to the outline that Laurie had given them over the
phone. It was modest fare by our general standards, but it was noticeably better
food than what the refugees were eating. They would not have wanted it any other
way. They were eating beans and rice and some other things, and we were given a
greater variety, and fish (a luxury, for sure), and most strikingly, there was may-
onnaise and a fresh bottle of ketchup and mustard for us, obviously purchased just
so we would feel at home.

It would be easy to rhapsodize about how this food — which is so different
than the Shabbat chicken I am used to and the sushi and fancy cakes and pastries
and ice cream and pizzas and Cajun-style fish and other things I can have whenever
I want — it is so easy to rhapsodize about how this meal held so much more
meaning for me than thousands of other meals I have eaten. People who know my
writing know that I am a romantic and given to exaggerate at times just to make a
point. But it is eight days later, and I have paused to recall the feelings I had while
sharing the food with the refugees, and I can see and sense now that I am *not* exag-
gerating, that the meal *was* tremendously moving, that the warmth of the hosts *was*
one of the most powerfully felt emotions I can recall *ever* in my life. We were all
touched by the efforts expended by the refugees for our benefit...these people who
have nothing, who have left their homes in desperation, who do *not* want to be
here, but would rather be in their homelands, living free, without fear of death,
torture, and hunger. (One of the Heroes had told us early on in our visit, "I don't
know of any of the refugees who *want* to be here.")

It would seem that the vast number of heroes down in The Valley are the
refugees themselves. I am not so naive as to think that they are all angels, but the
sense of sharing and giving for the benefit of others — and most of all their sense

of dignity — was a constant wonder to all of us who met them. Some of them have lost everything, but they have not lost their dignity

This insight was reinforced by the movie they showed us after dinner, an hour-long documentary made in El Salvador by a human rights group. As with "The Wrath of Grapes", it is all there in the film: the death squads, the *desapareci-dos* ("those who disappear"), the riots, bodies with bullet holes bloodied faces and pieces torn out of their flesh, the death of Oscar Romero, the Bishop murdered for his outspokenness on behalf of the rights of the people, the bodies of the four Catholic clergywomen being dug up, the interviews with government officials dou-bletalking and covering their bloody tracks....It's all there.

The enormous emotional conflicts weighed heavily on us: the movie screamed out that Life is Cheap. And yet, the refugees were surrounded by people who made it absolutely clear that that was not so. Life was indeed most precious in the eyes of their hosts. It was eerie watching the movie, and it was eerie trying to keep track of our emotions as we watched the movie and ourselves and the refugees all together as a group. We would never be the same as individuals. We were bound together now by catastrophe and suffering and the human struggle to emerge victorious over this great evil.

THE JEWISHNESS OF IT ALL

This refuge is in some faraway place in Texas that we would have never found on a map. There was a Never-Never-Land quality about the place, off a side road, through a gate, down a long path to a group of modest buildings set far off the road. We felt very far from "civilization".

When we arrived, we toured the refuge, and then sat with the members of the committee. We asked them questions, and they asked us questions. We asked about the refuge itself and about their struggles to reach the United States and about their families and their hopes and fears. They answered openly, eloquently, appre-ciative of the fact that we cared to ask. They were particularly impressed that we had come from so many places (Wisconsin, California, Louisiana, Washington, DC, New Jersey, New York).

But most of all, they wanted to know how it happened that a group of Jew-ish people arrived in their refuge to meet them, to hear them out, to dine with them on their hard wooden benches and tables. Many of them had never met Jews, oth-ers, at most, had some casual encounter with one or two of them.

They wanted to know why we had come down to The Valley.

We asked one of the Rabbis to speak. Andrew Warmflash volunteered. He explained how we Jews had been slaves in Egypt and had ourselves been refugees wandering forty years in the wilderness. It was a Biblical story familiar to all of them. Passover was still fresh in our minds, and the Rabbi called to mind many verses from the Torah about how one is not to mistreat the stranger, the outsider-coming-in, how we, as Jews, are commanded to remember what it was like to be oppressed, as we had been oppressed for some 400 years many centuries ago.

And the Rabbi explained that we were all children or grandchildren of refugees whose near-ancestors had fled Czarist pogroms and similar calamities, and that was not as long ago as the Exodus from Egypt, and that there are many, many Jews in the Soviet Union who wish to be free. And then he took up the theme of the Shoah — the Holocaust — and how one-third of our people had been murdered and how a million of them were children, and how the doors to so many countries were closed for us, including borders of the United States. Rabbi Warmflash was not comparing the enormity or the uniqueness of the Shoah to the Central American refugees' situation, but he was speaking of doors barred shut, which for us meant no place to go but to the Babi Yars and gas chambers and ovens.

We eight Jews had heard this theme time and time again as sermon material. We had nodded our heads, even seriously felt the needs of refugees around the world: our Ethiopian Jews, the Jews of the Soviet Union, Jews of Arab lands, people in Africa and Asia, and so many other places seeking refuge. But *here*, here in this refuge it finally sunk in...with full force.

There is so much similarity. The emotions of these Central Americans must be very much like what my grandfather felt in 1908 when he arrived at Ellis Island: questions and uncertainties, feelings of never going back home to Chorzele, Poland, to his house, his relatives. So, too, my grandmother, and my other grandmother, and my other grandfather's parents who came in the late 1880's or early 1890's.

We even said it to each other later on, we eight Jews — "There but for the Grace of God...."

I know the Jewish people has a long, involved agenda. We have so many, many things to take care of, and we all know how extensive the list is. Perhaps, had my friend Rabbi Feinberg never known of this work in The Valley, I, too, would have only considered the refugees in The Valley from a distance. Now I am "hooked". I am not throwing out the other items on the list of Jewish things to be involved in. By no means. I am just making a little more room in my free time and freeing some more spare money to include this very important Jewish problem.

I would hope other Jews would do the same.

REFLECTIONS VII

Jewish tradition indicates that it is a very great Mitzvah to raise orphans. Our ancient texts teach us that we may even sell our synagogues, all of the holy objects inside those precincts, even the holiest-of-holy object — the Torah itself — in order to provide for orphans.

In the modern-day Jewish community there are entire classes of people that feel orphaned, either because of embarrassment due to their personal circumstances or because the Jewish community has not yet aggressively reached out to them. My friend, Howard Feinberg, and I were on the phone one day, and I asked him to help me assemble a list of today's orphans. This is the result in no particular order of importance. It is, at best, an incomplete list:

Poor, hungry and homeless Jews, unemployed Jews, Jewish substance abusers (both alcohol and chemicals), Jewish battered spouses and children, Jewish elderly people, disjointed Jewish families (e.g., elderly people living far from relatives), homosexuals who are Jewish, Jewish AIDS victims, Jewish people dealing with catastrophic illness, Jewish people in need of hospice, Jewish people with physical, emotional and mental disabilities, surviving Jewish spouses, single Jewish parents and their children, Jewish latchkey kids, newly-arrived Jewish immigrants, intermarried couples, lonely Jews, unaffiliated Jews, Jewish college students, and Jewish adults who desire a Jewish education or a better Jewish education than they received as children but are too shy or embarrassed at this stage of life to ask for it.

So many groups.
So many individuals.
Such a large segment of the Jewish community in need of action by the Jewish communal establishment and by the Mitzvah heroes.

THE RABBANIT BRACHA KAPACH

It's The Rabbanit Kapach's faith that throws you off balance. Whenever you sit with The Rabbanit in her living room and talk about her Mitzvah work, she will always say things like, "HaShem Ya'azor-God will help" or "Be'Ezrat HaShem-With God's help."

But she is not a religious fanatic.

Let me give one example. I always visit her shortly after I arrive in Israel, sometime in June. The Rabbanit welcomes me and my friends and starts laying out the fruit and baked goods and something cold to drink. If it is a Friday morning, she will give me some home-baked pita bread for Shabbat, as the Sabbath is but a few hours away and she wants to honor me and my guests. She will add some S'chug, a green, fiery Yemenite condiment — her special dip for the pita. (Fiery is an understatement. It opens the pores, the sinuses, and just about everything else.)

June. It has been at least two and a half months since Passover when she had helped to provide food for about 2,000 families. She is still in debt from this Mitzvah project...more in debt than the worst credit card abuser's nightmare in America. As an annual ritual, I ask her how much she still owes for the Matzahs and flour and oil and other things she provided. Each year she quotes an ever larger figure. I continue the ritual and ask, "How are you going to pay off the debt?" And her annual reply is, "HaShem Ya'azor - God will help."

Early on in our relationship I used to be troubled, even angry at her for expressing such naive faith in God. I am hardly a person of such faith. I was raised in America in American surroundings, with a better-than-average Jewish upbringing...but nothing like this. I couldn't see how anyone could be so confident about God's gracious relationship with human beings, who believed it so gently, so inoffensively...and who lived life so meaningfully by that faith.

Now when I listen to her say it, I no longer humor her. She is so sincere about it; she may very well be right. She may have convinced me that this is the way God *really* works in the world. She's no peasant in some remote steppe in Russia or some primitive outback or bush where you might hear such phrases as an expression of the Simple Faith of the Simple People. No, The Rabbanit is very well educated, *very* bright, very knowledgeable in Torah (she teaches it regularly at an old age home, in other places to women's groups, in yet other places), and much more aware of the pain and suffering and very nature of human beings than I could possibly be. She is a very wise woman. Knowledge becomes wisdom through The Rabbanit; the words of our Jewish tradition are turned into a way of life that is filled with insight, warmth, and joy. She is *very* wise. I always go away from a morning with her thinking she knows something I don't know about God and The Universe and Life. It's just that at first it was difficult for me to comprehend; she and her life and theology were so different from mine.

BIOGRAPHICAL NOTES

The Rabbanit was born in Yemen about 60 years ago. When she was 11 years old she married a certain Yosef Kapach who is now one of Israel's pre-eminent Torah scholars. If you take two steps into his library downstairs you will get a hint of that — bookshelves so high you need not just ladders, but *high* ladders to get to some of the books.

She married Yosef Kapach at age 11 because he was an orphan and in those days in Yemen, Jewish orphans were grabbed by the government and forced to convert to Islam. The Rabbanit knows about the problems of teen-age marriage, so we joke about how she married so young so she wouldn't be a teen-age bride. (I have frequently wondered how I can sit there just joking around with someone who has been honored as a "Distinguished Citizen of Jerusalem". When you meet her, you will immediately sense her easygoing, unassuming nature, her humility.)

She gave birth to her first child at 14, and then had two more.

She was a grandmother in her 30's.

She and her husband came to Israel years ago, by donkey and then by boat. Here, too, we share some humor. I tell The Rabbanit she is probably making this all up because some time in the future I'll write up her story, and she'll want to put in some romance to her background, like donkeys from Yemen through broiling desert days and freezing nights. But that really is how she came to Israel.

She is — among many other things — a seamstress of rare skill.

And she is called "Rabbanit", which means "The Rabbi's Wife" (equivalent to "Rebbetzin" in Yiddish), but she is much more that just "someone-defined-by-being-married-to-someone-else."

I met her in one of my usual ways: more than a decade ago, Yitzchak Jacobsen, who co-ordinates my summer programs with United Synagogue Youth in Israel, said (read: *insisted*) I should meet her.

THE WONDER WOMAN OF NACHLA'OT

Many American children are growing up in TV neighborhoods besides their own real-live surroundings. They have Mr. Rogers' Neighborhood and the Sesame Street environment and other places television has provided them for their development towards maturity. I think it is safe to say that part of my own late growing-up took place in Nachla'ot, The Rabbanit's neighborhood in Jerusalem

Nachla'ot is a poor neighborhood, though you can clearly see some of the fanciest apartment buildings in Jerusalem from her apartment. Out her back window, beyond The Valley of the Cross and the ancient Monastery is the Knesset, the Israeli parliament building, and part of the campus of Hebrew University on Givat Ram. Next door, or down the block, or around the corner, though, are families — a multitude of families — in distress, in need of small or large or medium-sized Mitzvah efforts to keep them going.

Any hour of the day that I am with her, the phone rings. Some person or family has come up short and they need Bracha's help. (They call her "Bracha".) Anytime I am with her, the doorbell rings. Hushed conversations take place by the door, out of earshot. You could pick a thousand or ten thousand or a million human problems — The Rabbanit has heard them and worked to solve them. She is the equivalent of an entire social service agency in her neighborhood...and more. She is a most respected and admirable woman for what she does for others. In short, she is a Mitzvah hero as well as the equivalent of an MSW with four oakleaf clusters. And beyond all that, she is a pleasure to be with, to work with, to listen to. You can rely on her to work out both simple and incredibly complex human problems with great compassion and understanding.

No one is embarrassed to come to her with whatever difficulties they are experiencing at that moment. No man or woman or child that comes to her need feel ashamed that something has gone wrong, that there is not enough food for the Sabbath, that the children are having trouble in school, that work doesn't pay enough to provide a fair and decent mode of existence.

This point calls for some additional emphasis. As an American involved in many local Tzedakah projects, I hear over and over again that one of the problems in North American Tzedakah work is that people are too embarrassed to ask for help when they need it...even if they are in the most desperate of circumstances. They don't want to take charity. In that sentence, "charity" has a negative connotation. It means "a hand-out" and it suggests debasement, a lack of worth on the part of the one in need, i.e., for some reason the person-who-asks-for-assistance is viewed as not enough of a person to provide for himself or herself. Something has gone terribly wrong, and the victim ends up blaming himself or herself.

"Tzedakah" carries none of that weight. "Tzedakah" meaning "Justice" or "The Right Thing" simply signifies that something has, indeed, gone wrong, but no one is casting aspersions on the integrity of the person who needs an act of Tzedakah to set things right. "Tzedakah" means that the person-in-need is *entitled* to a response, and other people are instructed to respond. According to Jewish tradition, it is their obligation to respond. The Tzedakah-actor is not doing the other person a favor, and the situation is not defined as one of "helper" and "helpee". Someone "needs", someone else "has", and the one who "has" sets aright the imbalance by sharing with the one who "needs".

The Rabbanit Kapach responds because — as she understands her Judaism — God has instructed people to respond. In The Rabbanit's world, *everyone* is entitled to the good things in life, and if something has gone awry she — and anyone else she can teach and mobilize in her Mitzvah legions — will put out whatever time, energy, effort, and money that can be found to re-establish the person's balance. She expects no less of the people who come to her with their problems....They, too, are expected to do Tzedakah, to re-establish this balance of a decent life for others. No one gets off the hook, and no person who calls or comes to the door or opens the door when she comes to visit them is exclusively a recipient. They must be givers, too. With The Rabbanit there is no one-way flow of Mitzvahs. It is always bi-directional. Otherwise, where is the dignity of the situation, where is the grandeur of being human?

(I keep thinking of movies about crime bosses and how they always say to someone for whom they have just promised a favor, how they say, "Sometime in the future I may need a favor from you." There's always some heavy, ominous music in the background when The Godfather says it. What a contrast to The Rabbanit's two-way exchange!)

One article about The Rabbanit calls her the "The Angel of Nachla'ot". I'll temporarily demote her and only call her a Mitzvah Wonder Woman.

THE RANGE OF THE RABBANIT'S MITZVAH ACTIVITIES

Besides the throngs she manages for Passover, The Rabbanit has great numbers of families that enjoy a better Purim holiday because of her. Purim, celebrating the Jews' victory long ago over the evil Haman, must be a joyous day, so The Rabbanit is also in the Joy Business.

Plus working with the weekly needs for the Sabbath for so many families.

Plus setting up day camps in the Summer for neighborhood kids who would otherwise just hang-out and possibly get into trouble.

Plus managing every imaginable domestic problem: fighting, physical and verbal abuse, alcoholism, unemployment, in-law interference, catastrophic illnesses, deaths of spouses and parents and children, war injuries, orphans, psychological scarrings, difficult pregnancies and difficult births, physical and mental exhaustion, personality aberrations, heating and electric bills, phone bills.

Another plus: the small warehouse of used clothes in a big room underneath her apartment. Clothes and sheets and towels and blankets...lots of things.

Plus the swimming class. Here's where The Rabbanit's Mitzvah range comes into full play....When we think of Tzedakah, we so often think of food, clothing, shelter, medicine and the like. The Rabbanit goes beyond that. Take a harried mother with many children. Take the daily pressures of managing a household of that size with little reasonable opportunity for substantial financial improvement. Imagine the tension, the potential for feeling trapped. Thus, the swimming class for mothers. Mothers in this situation have to get out, to enjoy themselves, to feel refreshed. The Rabbanit arranged the class, but they wouldn't go unless "Bracha" would swim with them, too. (Did I mention that "Bracha" means "A blessing"?)

Plus the exercise class. One day I was with my friend, David Morris, at The Rabbanit's. We were sitting in the living room as usual, just sharing a few majestic moments with her. The doorbell rings. A woman comes to the door and insists that Bracha come with her down the block to the school building. The school year is over for the kids, so we have no idea what is going on. The Rabbanit takes us with her, and when we go inside, we see there is a party going on in the empty gymnasium. The same kind of women who swim with The Rabbanit are there, about 20 of them, and there are plates and plates of fine Oriental Jewish food laid out in front of them: chummous, techina, baba ganoush, salads, pita, fruits, nuts. It's the end-of-the-year celebration. Having concluded a season of exercise classes, these harried women (who at that moment hardly look harried) are having a party, and apparently blowing all the calories they burned off all year. They feel terrific, and from the moment The Rabbanit comes into the gym, you can see how much they love her. (Now that I think of it, besides admiring The Rabbanit, you find it very easy to love her.)

Plus the weddings. There are many aspects to her involvement in the Mitzvah of Hachnassat Kallah — providing-for-brides-and-young-couples-just-getting-married. There are a number of variations on her Hachnassat Kallah involvement:

The Rabbanit and her husband are pillars of Yemenite culture in Jerusalem and far out into the Hills of Judaea. On some evening before the wedding day, she makes certain that the Yemenite brides dress in the traditional Yemenite dress, a very exotic piece of clothing with chains of gold and bright colors and other things I can't begin to describe. (I leave you to see it for yourselves.) This Halbashat HaKallah ("The Dressing of the Bride") is a lively celebration, and she organizes such events throughout the year. Her presence is essential to any such celebration.

Indeed, there is a traditional Yemenite wedding dress in The Israel Museum in Jerusalem. The Rabbanit made it. (I mentioned she was an excellent seamstress.) And whenever there is an exhibition of Jews from Many Lands, it seems that The Rabbanit is the one who puts together the Yemenite display. There was a fine, fine evening a few years back at the President's Mansion, and my ticket of admission was the magic words, "I'm with The Rabbanit." She's even travelled to different countries, with trunks and suitcases loaded with the dress and the rest of The Travelling Yemenite Cultural Display.

That's only a small part of The Rabbanit's wedding projects, though. More important is taking care of brides and young couples who are starting out with nothing or nearly nothing. She is a Wedding-Dress Wonder Woman. She has racks of wedding dresses that people have donated, and I personally feel proud that I have managed to help gather a few for her. People going to Israel bring their wedding dresses and deliver them to her. Teen-agers coming on United Synagogue Youth Israel Pilgrimage bring wedding dresses. She gets them from everywhere. And that is how brides who would not have been able to buy one of their own (or even to rent one) can come to her, pick one out, get fitted, wear it, clean it, then return it to her for the next bride to use. All with the requisite lack of embarrassment. The Rabbanit is a Natural, and it is natural to go to her for things such as a wedding dress.

But she does much more. If they can't afford a dress, sometimes they might not be having a decent wedding. Once, during one of those many summers with The Rabbanit, she took me and one of my friends to a room a few blocks away for a small wedding. There were perhaps 40 people, maybe 50. It was a young couple whose parents had come from India. There had been family feuds, and there was little support from either side, and few family members would be attending.

Now, The Rabbanit doesn't go around helping people get married who ought not to get married. But she knew this particular couple well and saw that the marriage was a good thing, and so, without much support from the families, she made sure that there was a photographer, food, a Rabbi, *and guests*. Most of the people there were neighborhood people. How disappointing, how shameful it would have been if they would have gotten married with only a half-dozen people there.

Thus, the guests.

Including a couple of Americans tourists.

To make merry, to provide the all-holy element of Simcha, of Joy.

But it was the dress that made all the difference. I tried to imagine what the bride would have looked like with her soon-to-be husband, standing in front of a Rabbi with a couple of witnesses, standing there in an everyday dress. Seeing her in the magnificent gown that "someone, somewhere" had donated, you could see she had dignity. Married life would begin just right because of The Rabbanit. It was a privileged moment for me, a blessed day — that day those two people whose parents came from India to Israel and who had nothing in the way of material possessions to their name got married.

And with so many of these couples, there is need for more: sheets, towels, dishes, furniture, a set of knives, forks, and spoons. *Nice* furnishings and silverware. Things they would be proud to own and use. "Pride" in Hebrew is "Kavod", the same word for "dignity" and "self-image".

THE ESSENCE OF THE RABBANIT KAPACH

My sub-title is misleading. No one can capture the essence of The Rabbanit. Words are one step removed, as are photographs. She's short, she's lovely, she's gentle and humble, she's awesome-while-being-gentle-and-humble, she's easy to admire and love, she's as normal and natural as can be, she's playful, she's scholarly and wise. She's even what teen-agers in The Fifties would have called "cool". And though she only speaks Hebrew, everyone is able to communicate with her because of her unique personality.

The Rabbanit is on close terms with Teddy Kollek. Presidents and Prime Ministers and Members of Knesset know her well. She has her awards and prizes. But she doesn't need her awards and prizes....They're only a tool for more Mitzvah power.

The best way to capture the so-called "Essence of The Rabbanit" is to see her and to see her again; to take some stretch of time to be with her, to watch her as she interacts with all those hundreds of people she sees day-by-day, week-by-

The Rabbanit Bracha Kapach and a traditional Yemenite wedding head-dress.

Two USY Pilgrims model
wedding dresses
they brought to Israel for
the Rabbanit Kapach's brides.

week. There is much to be gained: a softening of the soul, a certain holy energy, faith.

If you want to capture her essence, the only way is to go meet her, to "hang-out" with her through a day that begins at 4:30 or 5:00 a.m., to listen to her and joke with her, to study Torah with her and see her faith in action. In sum: to apprentice yourself to her. Just call or write and set things up. Here are the address and phone number:

The Rabbanit Bracha Kapach, 12 Lod Street, Jerusalem, 249-296.

The Rabbanit holding cloth used to make wedding gowns.

REFLECTIONS VIII

The Talmud teaches us that there are 36 Righteous Ones in the world. They are known in Hebrew as Lamed Vavniks. Because of all the Evil and evils that exist in life, it is these 36 people who give God the patience to let our world endure. Their work, their being, sustains all humanity.

The Lamed Vavniks are Hidden Ones, unknown to other human beings. Mystery covers so much of the story of The 36. Indeed, in our ancient texts, there is no universal agreement as to the number of Hidden Ones (some say forty-five, some say thirty), but — 36 or more or less — they are known but to God. We mortals can only seek out other, visible Righteous Ones who somehow resemble The 36. I would imagine that the ones we discover have more human shortcomings than The 36, though there are also, no doubt, other differences. But by working with the Visible Ones, I believe we can stretch our imaginations to speculate about the nature of the Hidden Ones...perhaps.

One thing is certain: there are many, many more Second Level Righteous Ones than there are Hidden Ones. They are everywhere for us to see and to work with, if we but open our eyes to seek them out.

And there is yet another mystery about The 36: we have no teaching as to how a new Lamed Vavnik is selected when one of the existing 36 passes on to Paradise. Are some of the replacements chosen from the pool of the ones we know? Are they here already, alive, living quietly, unassumingly, and then eased into their new positions by Divine Word? In either event, is it our responsibility as Students of the Righteous to make certain there are potential replacements ready to assume their roles in the Grand Scheme of Things? Is that our job, to raise up a generation of possible Lamed Vavniks? And if we fall short, and there is no 36th One to fill the gap, what will happen to the world?

JOHN FLING

My instructions were to drive to Love's Chevrolet in Columbia, SC. One would hardly expect a pilgrimage to a Mitzvah hero to begin at a car dealership, but that was the starting point for my day with John Fling. Until recently he didn't have a phone, and the Chevy place had someone handling his calls: Vilma Fulmer, a great-grandmother, an associate and good friend of John's. Vilma retired recently, and John got a phone, but a few months ago when I first got to meet him, I just drove into the lot and found Vilma taking messages for John, calls from everywhere in Columbia, and West Columbia and Cayce and other remote areas on the outskirts of this Southern city. People needed things, but, even more, they needed John Fling.

John has been called "An Inveterate Samaritan" and "The Everyday Santa" by the newspapers. Reporters always need a good headline, something to catch the reader's attention, and both of these are good descriptions. But the headlines only tell part of the story, so I will try to record more of the details.

John Fling: 67 years old, raised in a sharecropper's house in Gabbettville, GA. Gabbettville is too small to be listed in the back of the road atlas, but I found it on the map. It's a few miles from the Alabama border in between La Grange and Lanett. John says there were about 40-45 people living there when he grew up, half of them his family. He is one of 19 children, and he says that's where he learned that you had to share things. He won't romanticize about his childhood; it was certainly not an easy one. He recalls his mother getting up before dawn and making 150 biscuits for the family every day, besides whatever else she could manage for breakfast and lunch and supper. He quit school after the fourth grade to help work in the fields. No, it was not an easy childhood, but from what I can gather, it was a great and loving household. Gabbettville is somewhere out there, and if I wanted to flesh out the story even more, I imagine I would do well to drive there someday.

The real story begins a couple of decades ago in Columbia, SC. John began to work delivering auto parts for Love's Chevrolet. He's now semi-retired or near-totally-retired, but the connection is still strong. The sales people and managers and mechanics and secretaries immediately recognized that this man was something out of the ordinary, and they became a part of his work.

His work: he takes care of just about everything for three kinds of people: children, people who are blind, and just about everyone else who finds him or whom he finds. Just plain folks. His kind of people. I think that is one thing about John that particularly attracts me to him: he is Southern and speaks very Southern and Country English. I am a Virginian, and while I hardly grew up in the backwaters or sticks of America, I could appreciate his manner of speech and the easy flow of words that never hid anything. There was no trickiness in his stories, no element of the shifty or slick. Everything was spontaneous, straightforward, and perfectly honest. Where others might say "mentally ill", he would just say "mental", and there were other similar words and phrases he used just like that one, but there are too many of them to record.

Vilma took me over to John. He was standing by his pick-up truck, loading second-hand clothes. It was about noon, and I had just driven in by Interstate 26 through vast rural stretches of South Carolina after a flight down from Washington. Driving up the state, I had plenty of time to consider who might be living a few miles east or west of the big highway and what they did in places in this country that seem like the middle of nowhere. John's people are people like that, and I'd meet more of them in one day than I would have met over many years of my "other" life.

The clothes: people give him clothes and he has a special permit from the city to set up a "clothes sale" (for free) anywhere he wants to. He just strings up a heavy cord against a tree or telephone pole, and people come to take what they need. They all know John Fling and they know there are no strings attached to anything he does. So they just come and pick out what they need until there's nothing left, and then he goes on to his next project.

Our first stop was to take this new load of clothes to one of his friends, who would sort the clothes and hang them neatly in preparation for the next "sale". The woman was in her 80's, just "plain folks", and bubbling over with pride that she'd be doing this kind of work for John. It was the most natural thing in the world for her.

That was my second encounter with John's People. The first was at the dealership, talking to Vilma and the owner of Love's and others who worked there. They all shared an enthusiasm for John's work. The next number of hours would be filled with similar reactions.

PLAIN FOLKS

NBC Nightly News had done a short feature on John's work which I had seen and taped. One scene is particularly poignant: John takes a bunch of his blind friends out to an old man's shack and shows them how they're going to paint it for him. Everyone is having fun, John as much as the rest of them. John took me down to meet the man who lived in that shack. He is pushing 90, in a wheelchair, and when I saw his house, I could tell it is was exactly that...a one-room run-down shack, complete with aging dog. But it wasn't really a shack from the outside. The paint job was wonderful, and John's appearance at the door filled the scene with a sense of glory. This was real human contact, and I can't help but think the man might have given up and died long ago, were it not for John's visits.

John shared some small talk with the man and gave him a lunch he had picked up at a restaurant on the way over. As soon as he had walked into the restaurant 20 minutes before, the people recognized John Fling and started dishing out the food into a styrofoam container. Sooner or later it would hit me that just about everyone around town knows John. It seemed quite natural that John would come into the restaurant that day or the next or the next one after that to pick up some food for this old man. The man wasn't an "old coot" or "codger". He was Some One, a person, and John made that point without saying it.

John Fling may not have much of a formal education, but he has a very quick human sense of things. He had probably never had a Jewish writer come down from Up North just to ride with him (though many people do come to see him and make the rounds). He certainly didn't know many people who had studied Talmud for a number of years. To tell the truth, it was a little eerie that he picked that old man for one of our first visits. It immediately triggered in my mind a certain Midrash, an ancient Jewish story about Moses. Not Moses the Grand Figure of the Exodus, but Moses the Shepherd living in exile in Midian, having fled Egypt because he had killed the Egyptian taskmaster. The story goes that one day a sheep ran away from the flock. Moses ran after it, found it drinking at some pool of water, realized that it had been thirsty, then picked it up and carried it back to the rest of the sheep.

Some people, myself included, would probably consider this bad management...leaving all the other sheep to pick up one lone stray. But the Midrash tells us that it was just that — Moses's concern for *every single sheep* — that moved God to select Moses as leader of the Jewish People. John Fling, a mini-Moses, did not differentiate between kinds of people. People are people, or, as he might say it, "folks are folks".

I would see many of these folks as I travelled around in John's pick-up. We'd stop by a house on a quiet road nowhere in particular and people would come out to the truck or he'd go inside and they'd talk about this and that and John would ask how things were and what they might be needing. And, if he could, he'd take care of it. There was a lot of talk about turkeys and hams and fixings because it was getting close to Christmas, so these were important items. It's really unfair to say that he'd be sympathetic. He was more than that. He was one of them and they knew they could share their innermost worries and fears with John. He'd understand. They would find relief one way or another, and they would never have to be embarrassed. On the surface it sometimes seemed they were just chatting, but something more was always going on through their words. John is a kind of psychological bank for them: they could deposit their worries with him and there would always be dividends. Having talked with Mr. Fling, they could sleep at night, knowing their lives were safe in his hands. Tragedies didn't seem so tragic; even catastrophies were not so catastrophic since John was there to listen.

In one such place John just came right in and you could tell that things had changed. It was already early evening and getting chilly, and there were a few people in the house. A mother and father and their friend and a few children. One child was very small for her age (she was 12 or 13), maybe weighing 20 pounds or so. You could apply all kinds of elaborate medical terms for whatever she was born with, but it was clear that the child had many complex problems, medical talk or no medical talk. It was a very intense scene. But when John picked the child up

John Fling advertises one of his "free" yard sales.

John with some of his kids.

and hugged her and talked to her and kissed her, all disease left the room; the chill in the air that overrode the heater was no longer such a problem, and the child was just a child... whatever the enormous medical complications might be.

I'll use the word again: it was glorious. It was more than just sublime. That very modest household (some would call it poor) was filled with what Jewish tradition calls "Tiferet" or "Pe'er", "Glory", "Incredible Magnificence". It was a feeling rarely captured in a house of worship. On the most basic level of all, I was saying to myself, "I am so glad to be alive to witness this moment."

Just plain folks and John.

All of them, just plain folks.

JOHN'S BLIND FRIENDS

I don't remember how Mr. Fling first became involved with blind people. I think someone from a local group for the blind had heard about him and called to see if he could drive some of them around. What's important is that he got started...and never stopped. And now there are all kinds of people in Columbia, SC, and environs who can't see but who know when John's in the neighborhood. I had read about one woman who went with her seeing-eye dog and John to the grocery store. The person at the check-out counter wouldn't sell her any dogfood because she had foodstamps. Foodstamp coupons are supposed to be for food for human consumption. John got the manager, but he also insisted it was against the rules. So John tore open the dogfood bag and started eating some of it, to prove that people could eat it as human-edible food. But the manager still wouldn't sell it to her....He just her gave the dogfood and was probably very relieved when John left. That was one story. Then we went to an apartment where there was a young couple about 35 or 40 years old...and a large, rather aged dog on the sofa. At first I thought it was just a pet, but it turned out to be their seeing-eye dog. I was used to sleek German shepherds, but, again, this day was so different from anything else I had known, I just added it to the List of Wonders. John chatted, as usual, then pulled the woman aside and said quietly that he knew she wanted to go home to her folks for Christmas and wanted to know how much the bus fare was. She estimated about $40-50, and he just took the money right out of his wallet and gave it to her. It didn't seem right to him that she wouldn't be able to go home to her family for Christmas, and since they were living on a bare subsistence income, *someone* would have to make sure she got home. (John, of course.) And there was no embarrassment. At no time during that day was anyone ashamed. No one.

You have to understand something about John and money. Since he's semi-retired, he told me he's not allowed to make more than $7,000 a year; otherwise it interferes with his Social Security income. But he empties his wallet all the time, and he's been doing it for years. I had told him early on that I had about $200 in cash with me for whatever he might need during the day. (I often ask people who buy my books at my lectures to overpay, so I can have some cash in a "slush fund" for various occasions. I had accumulated $200 from recent programs.) The money was John's for the asking. That was easy to do — it was other people's money. But when the day was over, and for weeks afterwards, I couldn't figure out why I didn't just empty my own wallet. I had about $100 in cash, and I was due in Charleston the next morning for some programs, and I could have easily used my credit card to get money or could have cashed a check at the motel. I *could have* done that, but I didn't. Two, maybe three months down the road I would do better, but at that moment, I was way behind John and just beginning to learn from him the meaning of Mitzvah money.

We went to someone else's home. When we came in, there was a smell of popcorn in the air. The young woman had just made a bag of microwave popcorn and shared it with me. She couldn't see me, but she knew that anyone that came around with Mr. Fling deserved to have whatever she could give. And that's why, after John coaxed her a little, she sat down to play the organ for us and to sing. (John had found her an organ.) The music and the singing were wonderful, touching higher spheres...and the microwave was more down to earth.

When we went back to the truck, John spoke about microwave ovens. He needed another one for one of his people. I had never thought about how convenient and practical and how much safer it would be for people who cannot see to have a microwave rather than use a gas or electric oven. That was a good cue for me to make notes, and I told him some of my friends would be able to get one for him....Which we did the next night in Charleston. I asked everyone in the audience to put in a dollar, and we'd send it off to John Fling for a microwave. We actually took in about $175, and the person who was going to send John the check would round it off to $200. What finally happened was that — at the reception afterwards — one of the members of the Jewish community pulled me aside and told me he'd get the microwave and John should use the cash for some other aspect of his Mitzvah work. It was a nice, special touch to the South Carolina trip.

As John drove me around town, he was always telling me stories. He has hundreds of stories, tales of woe and tales of high moments, tales of circumstance and illness and tragedy balanced or more-than-balanced by the right kind of active response. One of the stories is at once both irksome and joyous. It seems that he and one of his blind children were talking one day when John asked the little girl what she wanted. She said "A color TV." He asked her why in the world she would need a color TV. She told him that the sound always seemed to be better on color models, which made sense to John....so he got her a color TV. What happened next is so bizarre: someone down at the welfare office or some such place heard about what happened and wanted to deduct the value of the TV from the family's monthly payment.

This was too much for John. He pulled together some reporters and TV news people, picked up the TV, and took it down to the office. They wouldn't let him in, but he got in anyway and put the television on the supervisor's desk. The media had a field day, and people who saw or read the story responded as we might expect: stores merchants and private individuals gave her another TV. I think John said there were two or three or more of them in the final tally.

By the end of the day, I was getting tired. John was still moving from place to place, telling me it would take a week, at least, to cover his entire circuit. I wanted to get something to eat, and he said OK, but insisted that after dinner we would have to go back to one of the homes we had been in. I had to meet the rest of the folks. Earlier on we had met the mother, but her son and husband weren't home. He wanted me to meet the whole family.

It was about 8:00 p.m., and I was very tired and emotionally exhausted, but Mr. Fling wanted me to make this one last visit before I went back to the motel. We went back to this house and were welcomed by the family. I recognized the woman, met the husband, and saw their 16-year-old son on the couch. He was doing his homework. Though his mother was totally blind and the father's sight was restricted to an extremely limited range, the son had good vision. I don't recall that he even wore glasses. He interrupted his studies and talked about college while he took us on a tour of his fish tanks. He had an impressive collection of tropical fish and explained all the ins and outs of aquariums.

But John wanted me to meet the father. The story goes that one day the man told John his lawnmower was broken. He was hinting that John might want to try to get it fixed. John said, no, he wouldn't do that, but he'd get him an instruction book and he could fix it himself. What developed was a lawnmower repair shop in a shed in the back yard. (John may have been the one who got him the shed. Yes, I think it was John.) The man took me back there and told me all about his work. I have no mechanical ability whatsoever, so I asked elementary questions, and he spoke with authority. People from all around bring in their lawnmowers to repair, and the business brings in vital income for the family.

All along, as people hear me tell stories of John Fling, they think he is a man who just gives hand-outs. (I can see some Philosophers of Economics —and perhaps a few philosophically stingy people — baring their fangs and claws, ready to go for the jugular.) They miss the point completely. Wherever people need a microwave or a bicycle or medicine or cash or a rail ticket or something like that, *and there is absolutely no other way for them to get what they need*, and no one else steps in to be the provider, John steps in and provides it. But it is part of a package: the understanding is that everything is in a larger context, that no one gets away with being lazy or playing helpless. They all have to stand on their own two feet, to whatever extent they are able. The individual may be shaky with age or may have some sort of disability, but that doesn't take away their having to put out something from their own resources. And the mere fact that they cannot afford a nice Christmas turkey or ham doesn't make them no good. I found this so refreshing in the late 1980's when The Spirit of the Times made blaming the victim fashionable in many circles. The overworn and inaccurate "Why don't these lazy, shiftless people just go out and get themselves a job?" is way out of line when you travel with John Fling.

You know John's way of thinking when he tells you about his outings and picnics and shopping jaunts with the blind folks and the just plain folks. He's not interested in accusations and recriminations and blame for bare-subsistence living. Whatever John expects out of life, all his friends deserve to expect, and if that means he likes a nice day out in the park, that also means they get their nice day out in the park...with big baskets of food like anyone else would take with them on a picnic.

JOHN'S CHILDREN

I met Mrs. Fling, who shares John's vision of life, and I know they have children and grandchildren. Exactly how many there are I can't recall. But John's kids are really hundreds of children around town. He is a father to them, a grandfather, and uncle, a friend, everything a child might want at whatever stage of childhood they might be. Later on, 10 years or 20 years down the road, they will probably recognize him as a hero, but for now he is just a father, grandfather, uncle, friend, bringing them everything good childhood ought to have.

Just around when school was out for the day, John pulled on to a certain street and said, "Watch this." From houses all up and down the block, kids would appear. Small, very small, medium-size, and highschool-sized kids. They'd come running to the truck, he'd open the door, and they'd come over and give him a big hug. They'd talk about "things in general" and "nothing in particular" and then he'd go on to specifics, like how things are going in their particular family and with their specific schoolwork and all kinds of details about their own individual lives.

They weren't an aggregate or abstract class of people — "children in difficult domestic circumstances." He knew every one of them by name, by personality, by quirks, by hopes and fears. On that particular day, one of his projects was gathering kids for a special Christmas show at the civic auditorium. Someone had given him 19 tickets, and he told one of the kids to find the other 18 to come with him for the program. He named a few names and told them they should dress up nice, and to be sure to be ready by such-and-such a time of day so he could pick them up.

This happened again and again as he combed the streets and talked with the children. In other places at other times, parents might be justifiably suspicious and wary of some man in his 60's driving up and talking to their kids and offering them goodies. On the surface it sounds like the insidious Candy Man and kidnappings and molestations and other nightmares we read and hear about. What a refreshing change this was! And often (if they were home) the parents would come out to talk with John, too.

In between stops he'd tell me about the families: a father doing 18 years in prison, parents who are alcoholics or addicted to pills, four families living in one house, a long-unemployed mother, kids dumped with grandparents, abandoned, 5 or 6 kids from 5 or 6 different fathers, families going through plain old hard times.

John says, "They just have to know someone loves them", which is a fair summary of what John means to them.

I will have to go back to Columbia sometime on a Sunday. Sunday mornings, starting out very early, John picks up kids for church. He has a new van that holds about 15 people, given to him or leased for one dollar or something like that by the dealership. He fills up the van with a load of kids and takes them to church with a stop at a doughnut shop on the way where the owner gives them something to drink and some goodies. I think he makes two or three rounds like this on Sunday mornings.

That's one of the reasons why these kids don't fall into bad ways. That's why you don't hear much about a half-dozen foster homes for each kid. Everything is working against them except for one critical factor: John Fling. He's like the best youth group advisor anywhere. As long as they have their Mr. Fling, they don't need all those other avenues of escape that are waiting to snare and destroy kids like them in other cities. So he is a father, grandfather, uncle, friend, and youth group advisor, though there's no formal club called "John's Kids"... but all the kids know they're a part of the club.

TIME FOR HIMSELF

Some people might think, "Lord, when does he ever get time for himself?" That is certainly a fair question, but I think it misses the point: everything John Fling does is his Time for Himself. He is not selfless; he is All Self. John Fling neither has nor wants leisure. He's tired, for sure, but he *wants* to be tired, whether it's taking his kids out for a movie or expecting the Good Lord to help find him the money to get another microwave or kid's wagon or getting a color TV for a little blind girl, one of his friends.

You may study his life to see what exactly got him going, what incident or lifestyle from his childhood or adulthood set him on this path of Mitzvah work. You might screen him or grill him to look for hints of phoniness (there is none, *absolutely* none of it), but, in the end of all the searching, there is a final mystery. For whatever reason in the world he does it, this is what he does, and this is who he is.

John Fling has seen great sadness in his work, but the sadness does not beat him down. He sees unimaginable hardships and injustices every day, but here, too, he takes on injustice and hardship and poverty and sorrow and grinds them fine in his soul, and they somehow emerge docile and harmless. He lightens so many human burdens, turns so much sadness to joy. Others might take all this intensity — this enormous human frustration he encounters — and smash every plate and glass in the house or shoot wildly with a gun at anything that moves.

Not John Fling.

His is a most blessed life, and whether or not I or anyone else is envious of his life is irrelevant. It is enough just to ride with John and take in the glory of it all.

John Fling, POB 2144, Cayce W. Columbia SC 29171. Phone: 803-256-7195 or 803-360-JOHN.

REFLECTIONS IX

King David: shepherd, slayer of Goliath, Psalm-singer, conqueror of Jerusalem, descendant of Ruth, father of Solomon.

And yet, for all that, not allowed to build The Holy Temple.

Two interpretations are usually given for why the Lord did not want David to build The Temple, both reflecting the phrase, "there was blood on his hands": (1) He had been a warrior, perhaps too much a warrior, and this clashed too blatantly with the symbolism of The Temple, a haven of peace, and (2) in order to marry Batsheva, he had sent her husband, Uriah, into battle to be killed.

One Jewish text offers a third interpretation (Yalkut Shimoni, Ruth 603):

On the day that David killed Goliath, all the women were so ecstatic, they threw all their gold and silver at him. He solemnly set the treasure aside for the building of The Temple.

Later, when he was King of Israel, there was a three-year famine. The people came to him for aid, but he refused to release that money to feed the people.

The Holy One said to David, "Since you did not accept the responsibility to give the people their lives, I swear that Solomon, and not you, shall build the Temple."

SISTER MARGARET McCAFFREY

A number of years ago I spoke in Shreveport, LA. The Jewish community down there had me address a women's group of about 150 people. When the program was over, some of the women introduced me to their special guest, Sister Margaret. It was obvious that she was their Mitzvah hero.

Since the vast proportion of my Tzedakah work takes place within the Jewish community, this was something relatively new for me. It reminded me of stories of Jewish people helping Father Flanagan in his early days of establishing Boys Town in Omaha. Imagine....All these Jewish women talking about a nun!

Sister Margaret and I only had a few minutes together, but we stayed in touch through the mail, and my Tzedakah fund would occasionally channel some money to her Christian Service Program. She had some wonderful endorsements. Finally, a few months ago, Shreveport's Jewish community invited me back for some more talks. This was my chance to see Sister Margaret at work.

One of my souvenirs from the recent visit to Sister Margaret's turf is a cartoon from the local paper. The first few frames show someone speaking with the Mayor of Shreveport who is bragging about the fact that the city has a "collective social conscience". He continues with, "We...look after our under-privileged", and explains that the city's commitment to poor people is "simple, yet effective." The other person asks, "How does it work?" In the final frame, a nun picks up the phone and answers, "Yes. This is Sister Margaret. Can I help you?"

There's lots of irony in the cartoon. So much of what Sister Margaret has to do should be handled by various branches of local, state, and federal government agencies. But, while that's all being worked out — if it is being worked out at all — *someone* has to take care of the people.

In the cartoon, Sister Margaret is wearing a habit, with a Supernun cape draped over the back. A wonderful touch; she really is Supernun.

In real life Sister Margaret doesn't wear the elaborate habit we frequently associate with women in a specific Catholic order. She certainly doesn't parade her commitment to her religion, nor does she thrust it upon anyone else. I could tell that even in the first few moments when we met six or seven years ago.

(It happened again. I just called Shreveport to ask Sister Margaret for a picture for the book. She was out of town, but one of her assistants told me about some new projects going on. I told the woman that it is hard to write a book when you keep calling up your heroes and you just want to drop everything and get back to work with them.)

Now I was back in Shreveport, and the town and its people were suffering. They have been badly hit by plunging oil prices. It is hard times for many people.

I sat with Sister Margaret and one of her friends and the Director of the Jewish Federation and Helaine Braunig, a friend from Shreveport who is very involved in Mitzvah work. We were at the place where Sister Margaret feeds people, a kitchen and dining room arrangement, simple, clean, and ever-so-important to the hungry people who come to eat. I told her that it was good to be back with her, and I wanted to tour her various projects.

As we walked around the office of the Christian Service Program and other buildings she is renovating for shelter and other programs, she sounded like the Greatest Builder in the World displaying with pride the latest shopping center or skyscraper the company had put together. It's the same kind of thing....just different kinds of building.

The extent of what Sister Margaret accomplishes daily really awes you. But as much as how much she does, it's the quality of the work and her special touch that makes all the difference. For example: clothes. When people need clothes, the rooms where they are kept are laid out neatly, just like a store. Everything is on racks by size, all the shoes on shelves like in a regular shoe store. It caught me off guard at first, but I later knew I should expect such treatment from Sister Margaret.

Besides food and clothing, there are enormous utility bills to help pay. Sister Margaret's assistant says there will be a free medical clinic soon, and a shelter for women and children is in the works. And three more nuns are coming down soon to work with Sister Margaret.

The people who come to Sister Margaret for her magic touch are quickly set at ease. Whatever bureaucratic runarounds and humiliations they might have been through before getting to The Supernun of Shreveport, they get none of that with her. No one is a "case", no one a "client". They are people, some of them living on a most precarious edge, and if it is in her power to take care of them, she will most certainly do whatever is possible.

I have a January 1-June 30, 1987 semi-annual report from the Christian Service Program. A few specific items will give you a better perspective on the extent of what she does:

Donations from Individuals - $235,633.76
Donations from Organizations - $53,262.91.

(Sister Margaret's program is very much a people-for-people network. She does not focus on grants from foundations, though I am sure she would most certainly welcome an expert in grant-writing to help her out.)

Disbursements:

Food	$ 24,510.30
Utilities	116,126.26
Medical care	28,885.20

(Self-explanatory.)

Operating expenses (I select some salaries):

	953.05	
	900.00	
	8,078.51	(2 salaries)
	1,285.87	
	400.00	
Telephone Room Supervisor	96.00	

(I kid Sister Margaret that she's only in it for the money.)

Total Disbursements	322,529.57	
Total Receipts	293,063.73	
Cash Balance	12,976.74	[A *balance*?]

(If you didn't know the program had some money in the bank before January 1st, you would wonder how $293,063.73 minus $322,529.57 leaves a plus $12,976.74. You might suspect a miracle of some sort.)

One incident that happened when I was in Shreveport helps the budget make more sense. My hosts had put me in a very nice motel. Early one morning I took a walk, passing a small shopping center on the way. On the way back I saw a small French bakery just opening up, so I stopped in for coffee. I had heard about and read about people who pick up day-old bread from bakeries and drop it off at some Mitzvah project. I had even met a few of them (they are described elsewhere in this book), but I had never tried it myself.

I asked the person behind the counter what they do with bread they can no longer sell. (I couldn't believe I had actually asked.) The woman answered that the Salvation Army used to come pick it up, but they no longer do so. I explained that I was going to see Sister Margaret at lunchtime, and would she mind if we came by and took some of it to her? The woman was delighted and pointed out three huge bags of French bread and pastries that were ready for the dumpsters. Some of the baked goods might need to be heated in an oven for a few minutes, but it was all edible. The sacks must have weighed 150 or 200 pounds in all and were certainly worth a few hundred dollars. It was as simple as that, and I realized it really wasn't so hard to ask.

And since the Braunigs lived near the bakery, and since one of them worked near where Sister Margaret's program is located, a weekly pick-up and delivery was arranged. As simple as that...a few minutes on the way to work, a few minutes out of the way once downtown, and many more people would be enjoying fine French bakery items.

Local people who think in those simple terms (emptying the closet more, rather than less, frequently, emptying their kids' toychests more, rather than less, frequently, cleaning their wallets more, rather than less, frequently) are the mainstay of Sister Margaret's work.

Sister Margaret has been in the very thick of this kind of Mitzvah work for years. She's 60 years old and she mentioned (with a childlike smile) that people are beginning to ask who will eventually take over this work. I informed her that Jewish tradition gives people 120 years on earth, so she is just beginning to get into high gear.

I could describe Sister Margaret more fully if you wanted, but to a Jewish boy from Arlington, Virginia, she looks like every other 60-year-old nun he's ever seen. She *is* gentle, she *is* compassionate to the Nth degree, she *is* warm and friendly and unassuming and humble, and while her vows have set her free of worries for material goods, what *really* counts in her world is that *she is what she does.*

If you want to know her, you must watch her at her holy work.

Sister Margaret McCaffrey, c/o Christian Service Program, POB 21, Shreveport, LA 71161, 318-221-4539.

Sister Margaret McCaffrey.

REFLECTIONS X

Statistics, statistics. Some crazier than others.

"Harper's Index" from Harper's Magazine. Numbers as of September 1987 (and I quote):

1. Amount the Pentagon budgeted for Star Wars research in 1987: $3,500,000,000.

2. Percentage of highschool students who say the telephone was invented after 1950: 10.

3. Number of public officials charged with corruption by the federal government in 1986: 916.

4. Price of a .44 Magnum pistol issued to commemorate the Constitution's anniversary: $1,295.

5. Amount paid at auction for the hunting permit to kill one bighorn sheep in Montana in 1987: $109,000.

Jerusalem Post, July 24, 1986 (a Reuters wire story from New Delhi):

At least 1,672 Indian women were killed over dowry disputes in the past 2 1/2 years. The last year's statistics jumped to 855 women, up from 534 in 1984.

"Many victims are killed by being doused with kerosene and set alight."

More from "Harper's Index" (a month later than numbers above):

1. Price of Pet Rest — a casket, bodybag, sympathy card, and memorial-service text — for a guinea pig: $14.99.

2. Number of direct-mail solicitations sent to Henry David Thoreau at Walden Pond this year: 90.

3. Value of the toys the average American child received as gifts in 1986: $200.

A crazy world. Different categories of numbers, different realities behind them all.

All strung together, a crazy world.

SKETCHES

I. PEOPLE I HAVE MET

DANIEL KUTTLER

Daniel Kuttler (may his memory be for a blessing to all of us) was a dear human being. "Dear" used to carry more weight in English; it meant "precious", "of great value" with overtones of nobility. "Teuer" in Yiddish and "Yakar" in Hebrew still have those connotations, and Yiddish and Hebrew were passions of his. When we think of Dan, we should think of all those added meanings.

A number of years ago his nephew, Sandy, called, insisting that I meet his Uncle Dan and Aunt Charlotte on my next summer trip to Israel. People do that frequently with me, knowing I am on the look-out to meet heroic individuals, and I usually leave for Jerusalem with a list of 15 or 20 of them, hoping to find time to see a few. I never seem to get to all of them, though. But Sandy was an old friend, and he was persistent, so meeting his aunt and uncle became a priority. I am grateful that he pushed so hard.

Daniel Kuttler was passionate about many things in life — he was no mere passer-through, no distant observer. His soul's energy flowed wherever there were Mitzvahs to be done, all kinds of Mitzvahs. But he had a particular passion: young couples about to get married. He and Charlotte became The Wedding Dress People, gathering gowns from friends in America and other places, racks of them, and fitting out the young brides who might otherwise not have been able to buy one or rent one. The brides would come into their apartment on Keren HaYesod Street, and, without the least shred of embarrassment, pick a dress they would want to wear, be fitted for it, wear it, and then return it after the wedding.

How many brides were there in all? It would be hard to say, but there are albums and albums of pictures. This wedding and that one and the next one, pictures of the Kuttlers as honored guests, Dan and Charlotte smiling with a bride, sometimes an orphan, sometimes someone with just about nothing material to her name.

It wasn't always wedding dresses, of course. I am sure there are hundreds of little and big things that go along with starting married life that the Kuttlers helped find for the brides and grooms: bedding, other household items, all kinds of things. I never once got a sense that any of the young women were "just another bride". Each time Dan and Charlotte would take out the albums there would be a story to tell, but not just a story....when the albums were out, their enthusiasm grew. These were no longer just pictures or stories but people, people with nearly nothing, but, because of Dan and Charlotte, people with everything real in life, love, caring, concern, passion-for-life, hope.

I first met Dan when he was in his 60's, and it struck me that this must be a great way to stay young (or to grow old, depending on your perspective), going to weddings, and, of course, baby namings and circumcisions and all kinds of other ceremonies.

How many weddings were there? A couple of hundred? More? Less? How many years of dancing at these events, performing the Mitzvah of Bringing Joy to the Bride and Groom with authentic, deep, blessed joy?

Now, there are people who perform Mitzvahs coldly, mechanically, automatically — it is God's will, this thing called Mitzvah; it must be done because it is a commandment. But there is no joy in the way some of the people would perform the Mitzvah. Dan would have none of that. Never cold, never mechanical or automatic. Quite the opposite....He was always pleasant and dear, particularly when performing Mitzvahs.

Although it might seem to be a contradiction in terms, I imagine there are even people who perform this particular Mitzvah of Bringing Joy to the Bride and Groom mechanically and without any heart. Sometimes you can pick up on an undercurrent of sadness in the heart that breaks through the Simcha, the Joy, and the underlying sadness spoils the Simcha. Joy without Joy. Dan would have none of that. He was never mechanical or automatic in his joy — no matter how many weddings he adorned with his unique presence. Certainly there was never any joy-burdened-with-sadness. Dan Kuttler's joy was pure.

This joy spilled over into the rest of his Yiddishkeit, his Jewish way of living; it was in his prayers, in the way he ate a meal on the Sabbath, in the way he talked Torah with his guests. He never imposed his Orthodoxy, never pushed you. Sitting in his living-room-dining-room, you found yourself attracted to him and to all he was. It wasn't what he represented that drew you to him, because he wasn't a symbol of anything: he *was* someone, a very alive person, a very Jewish person, which I sense now might be synonymous.

I last saw Dan in the summer of 1987. I was walking on King George Street, and he was coming down the sidewalk, returning from synagogue. He looked thinner and weaker than usual, and he moved more slowly than normal. I had heard he had been in the hospital but had no sense that things were quite so serious. We chatted, then moved on.

A couple of months ago I got one of his regular letters, typed and mimeographed, the letters he mailed to his friends who wanted to know what Mitzvah work he was up to and how they could channel their Mitzvah efforts through him. This is the content of that letter, exactly as he wrote it from Miami where he and Charlotte spent a few months every year:

To My Dear Family and Friends:

Writing this letter won't be an easy one for me. When I left Jerusalem to come here, I felt sure my charity efforts and all our

Mitzva work, was over. I was very happy just to be able to come here.

When I came, I became aware of how much better and easier it was for me to breathe. The climate of course helped and within a short time, my health improved considerably. I was able to resume most of my usual activities, like walking and my daily attendance of Synagogue Service to which I of course was very grateful to Hashem.

These were things I prayed for and G-d must have heard and answered. The thought came to me that evidently "He" wanted me to continue in the beautiful work we do in Israel, so "He" gave me the strength to continue. I am truly grateful.

Now, with your help, we hope to continue our Mitzva work with Poor Brides and Poor People, as long as I am able. I hope I can count on you again for your support and we promise to use it to the best of our ability.

Hopefully I will be able to write to you of the nice and interesting things we do in Israel.

G-d bless you for your generosity.

Sincerely,

Charlotte and Daniel

The letter arrived about a week after Sandy called me to tell me Daniel Kuttler had died. Charlotte sent a cover letter explaining that he had written it two days before he fell ill and passed away.

A long time back, maybe twenty years ago, I learned a story in the Talmud about the death of Rabbi Judah the Prince. He was deathly ill. The Rabbis sent one of their colleagues, Bar Kappara, to see how Rabbi Judah was faring. When Bar Kappara saw that Rabbi Judah had died, he reported back to the Rabbis with the following words, "Both angels and human beings took hold of the Holy Ark. The angels have overcome the mortals and the Holy Ark has been taken captive."

How apropos for the life and passing of Daniel Kuttler. All those people on earth, all those brides in particular, struggled and prayed that he would live on, continuing far into the future with his divine mission of Mitzvahs. But the heavenly powers won out. Dan Kuttler and The Holy Ark — they both contained the Torah. In the Ark is a Torah of parchment and ink, inanimate, that waited for a Dan Kuttler to bring it to life.

THE PEOPLE OF BET TZEDEK

There is a crowded office on Fairfax Avenue in Los Angeles, in the heart of a Jewish neighborhood. It is an energetic place and, I believe, a very holy place. It is the office of Bet Tzedek, and in the offices and hallways and the waiting room, poor people have their legal problems solved, free of charge. It is the Pro Bono Kingdom.

I have heard about the Bet Tzedek people, read about them (I have their 1985 Annual Report and recent newsletters), and I have gone to see them.

Their facts and figures are rather staggering:

In 1985, they helped more than 8,000 low-income clients.

By 1985, their budget had grown to $1,500,000. Funding comes from private contributions, the County of Los Angeles, and many other sources.

In 1985, there were more than 100 volunteer attorneys working for Bet Tzedek (though some staff members now receive a salary).

In that year, the volunteers provided more than $2,000,000 worth of legal work.

Bet Tzedek has a most impressive staff of attorneys and paralegals. Some of the people who work there are retired from legal practice and judgeships, some have thriving private practices of their own, and others work for large firms or corporations.

More than half of all the legal work performed by Bet Tzedek is carried out by volunteer attorneys, paralegals, and law clerks.

And I quote, "In all, more than 89 percent of all completed Bet Tzedek cases had an outcome favorable to our clients."

Then there is their extraordinary expansion of programs throughout the area, with particular outreach to elderly people...including mobile attorneys and paralegals doing "house calls". More than 70% of their clients in 1985 were 60 years of age or older. They have a Nursing Home Advocacy Project (NHAP), preserving the rights of residents and handling cases of abuse and mistreatment.

They win awards all the time and from all quarters.

They have won some landmark cases. Most well known is *Grunfeder vs. Heckler,* a five-year-long court battle on behalf of a disabled Holocaust survivor. The issue was denial of SSI benefits because Bet Tzedek's client was receiving reparations payments from West Germany. Bet Tzedek took on the Social Security Administration and won, bringing relief to thousands of survivors who receive token reparations money from West Germany.

Their history is also reasonably staggering: in 1974, what seemed like an insignificant number of Jewish attorneys got together to begin doing *pro bono* work on behalf of needy clients in the neighborhood.

Now they reach far beyond the neighborhood.

Now they are not a seemingly "insignificant number" of attorneys. The modest office space of 1974 has expanded, though they could use even more space.

And now there are non-Jewish as well as Jewish attorneys, and non-Jewish as well as Jewish clients. Clients and visitors hear many languages in the hallways and offices and waiting room.

The story of Michael Feuer, the director of Bet Tzedek, is equally engrossing: Harvard undergraduate. Harvard Law School graduate. Corporation work and work on political campaigns. Tall, handsome, the whole nine yards. (Did I mention that when I met him he wasn't yet 30 years old?) A man on his way up the ladder of success.

The tone and tenor of Bet Tzedek: Kavod — dignity everywhere. Tzedek — justice everywhere. Tzedakah — righteousness, doing the right thing everywhere. A sense of Mitzvah — doing good things...everywhere. (Indeed, there should be places like Bet Tzedek everywhere.)

One particular case I was following is my personal favorite, The Cadillac Hotel. It took four years, two lawsuits, and hundreds of staff and volunteer hours to win, but Bet Tzedek won. The Cadillac Hotel is in Venice, California, on the boardwalk. Its tenants are low-income elderly people. The landlord attempted to evict the tenants in order to renovate the building and turn it into a luxury hotel, overstepping his legal bounds in the process. That is where Bet Tzedek came in four years, two lawsuits, and hundreds of volunteer hours ago. This is part of the settlement (I quote from the Bet Tzedek newsletter):

1. The current residents of the Cadillac may remain in the Hotel for the rest of their lives, at their current, very nominal rents (averaging $100 per month).

2. Each current resident receives a substantial cash payment, or household furnishings of equivalent value.

3. Numerous repairs will be made to the tenants' rooms and the Hotel in general, from a new elevator to refurbished bathrooms.

4. If, in the course of these repairs, any tenant finds the work too disruptive, the tenant will be temporarily relocated by the owner, at his expense, and returned to the Hotel when repairs are completed.

5. If a tenant is temporarily relocated more than 300 feet from the Israel Levin Community Center — the focal point of the tenants' cultural, religious, and social life — the owner will provide round-trip transportation, twice a day, for the duration of the relocation period.

6. Former residents of the Hotel receive substantial cash payment, as do estates of deceased former residents.

7. A major cash contribution has been made by the owner to Bet Tzedek's Conciliation Services program.

Number 5 is my favorite.
There *is* Justice in the World.

Bet Tzedek, 145 S. Fairfax Ave., #200, Los Angeles, CA 90036, 213-939-0506.

REUVEN MILLER AND SI LEVINE

Simple and brief: Reuven Miller is my age and has 11 children (one girl, one boy, seven more girls, another boy, another girl; he jokes that the pattern is simple — every eighth child is a boy). He makes a living at a printing business he owns, has a noticeably severe reading disability, and does Mitzvah work all the time.

About 15 years ago in Boston Reuven's Mitzvah network began to grow. He would get calls and more calls. He set up a small Tzedakah fund called the Ohel Chesed Charity Fund.

Now he's in Baltimore, picking up on Mitzvah work there while keeping up with the Boston project by phone and letter.

There's not much more to tell. He's a lovely man. He operates very quietly in the world of Mitzvahs and puts very great faith in God's ability to help provide the means to help him do the Mitzvah work at hand.

And he's a very good friend of mine.

When I asked him whether or not I should mention him in the book, promising not to over-praise him or embarrass him, he said "Sure!" That's not "Sure! I need to have my ego stroked." That's "Sure! if it will get me more support for the Mitzvahs."

With Si Levine there's also not much to tell. He's across the ocean, having moved from Cleveland over a decade ago to settle in Jerusalem. He's in his mid-70's and continues doing what he used to do for years back in Ohio: Mitzvahs. Si worked in the public school system for a long time. He was also active as an advisor for Jewish youth groups, and I rarely go any great length of time without someone telling me he or she was influenced by Si from the days they were kids in Central Region United Synagogue Youth. Many former teen-agers are now grown-up active, committed Jews because of Si's years with USY.

"On the side" he was doing time-and-a-half Mitzvah work.

Reuven and Si both remind me of the Talmudic story about Binyamin HaTzaddik (Bava Batra 11a). All three — Binyamin, Reuven, and Si — had Tzedakah funds at their disposal. Once, centuries ago, a woman came to Binyamin and said she needed food. Otherwise she and her seven children would die of starvation. At that moment there was no money in the Fund, so Binyamin HaTzaddik fed her out of his own pocket.

Si and Reuven would do the same, and no doubt have done the same many, many times in the past.

I suppose that's a little more than "not much to tell".

Reuven Miller, 6505 Western Run Dr., Baltimore, MD 21215, 301-358-3261.
Si Levine, 23 Horkania St., Jerusalem, 666-864.

REB OSHER FREUND

Some Mitzvah work simply transcends all factionalism. When a very orthodox individual is recommended to me by someone who is not a part of that environment, it is a sign that something spectacular may be happening.

In 1961 I stayed in Jerusalem at the Ron Hotel in Zion Square. I was a teen-ager, a participant in the United Synagogue Youth Israel Pilgrimage, and this was our home base. The owner, Yehoshua Lendner, was our friend. When I returned to Israel in 1964, we picked up where we had left off, and when I began to return annually in the beginning of the 1970's, each year I would go back to the Ron and visit.

One year, Yehoshua suggested I meet Reb Osher Freund. Yehoshua apparently had been helping out with some of Reb Osher's projects (called Yad Ezrah) and thought it would be beneficial for me to see the man responsible for so much Tzedakah activity. We got in the car and rode around from one part of Jerusalem to another as people told us he was probably here or there or somewhere else. Finally the connection was made, and I have since enjoyed a number of years as a student-of-Mitzvahs of Reb Osher.

Reb Osher *is* a part of the ultra-Orthodox community, but his vision and Mitzvah projects do not differentiate between one person and another. I still feel a little jumpy — for any number of reasons — when I meet people who display such a deeper commitment to their Judaism. Meeting Reb Osher was disarming, though. He radiated a gentleness I have rarely been privileged to experience. His face, his words, his manner...all kindness. His presence and manner brought to mind the Talmud's words (Megillah 31a), "Wherever you find God's awesome power, there, too, you will sense His gentleness." This seems like a contradiction in terms — power and gentleness combined. But when I met Reb Osher, it became clear that his awesome Mitzvah power derives neither from some hereditary position nor from a physically authoritative bearing, but rather from his exquisite gentleness. Yad Ezrah's multitude and scope of programs, it's marvellous growth and success, can be traced back to this quality of Reb Osher's. Gentleness and power are an all-too-rare combination, so knowing Reb Osher has been particularly rewarding for me personally.

Reb Osher's son, Avremel, who appears to be about my age, recalls that when he was a child, he would go with his father to deliver fruits and vegetables to people in need. Avremel is still intimately involved in his father's Tzedakah work, but the projects now extend far beyond food deliveries. For the year 1986-1987, these are some of the numbers: 12,300 people made use of Yad Ezrah's low-cost dental clinic (3 more clinics are being set up), 700 people a week receive Shabbat food packages, an old-age residence with room for 98 people is nearing completion, a 60-unit housing complex for poor people is being built, 26 weddings for poor couples were prepared at Yad Ezrah's kitchens, 585 children of families in difficult financial circumstances attended 7 day-care centers, 500 elderly people a day received warm meals at various Yad Ezrah programs, 600 people were enrolled to make use of Yad Ezrah's five discount supermarkets, 98 people worked in their sheltered workshops for individuals with mental disabilities, and 76 students studied at Ohr Yerushalayim, their special education facility.

The special workshops are among my favorites because of the results they have achieved. Two of the workshops — a sewing workshop and a printing press — take in people from Jerusalem's mental institutions and other individuals from their homes. If I did not know Yad Ezrah's specific approach, I would have expected something radically different: emotional outbursts, thick tension in the workshops, tranquilizers to calm the people. Some of the people who come to work there have severe emotional and psychological difficulties. But the atmosphere is decidedly *not* tense, I have not seen hysterical outbursts, and I don't know of any Yad Ezrah supervisor that administers any tranquilizing drugs to the workers. The supervisors, true students of Reb Osher, have his gentle touch and utter devotion to the welfare of others, and this loving supervision creates an atmosphere of calm and hope.

It might (perhaps) be unfair to say that gentleness and love are much better for an aching psyche than the finest medicines. Perhaps. But if this is only a "perhaps", how do we account for the fact that Yad Ezrah manages to re-integrate a much-higher-than-to-be-expected percentage of its people back into the "normal" flow of society? Why are the numbers, the "bottom-line success rate", so impressive? Yad Ezrah's methods should certainly be studied very closely, with all the latest scientific tools of observation.

And still I feel that more ought to be said....With more than 100 pages finished on this topic of Mitzvah heroes, I feel comfortable stating The General Rule of Mitzvah Heroes:

Because of the Mitzvah Hero's very nature and quality-of-insight, more can be accomplished in any specific Mitzvah area than by conventional means, much more.

And a Corollary to The General Rule:

By learning from and working with Mitzvah Heroes, Conventional Mitzvah People can surely expand the range and depth of their own Mitzvah work.

And a Second Corollary to The General Rule:

Conventional Mitzvah People may, quite possibly, rise to truly awesome, heroic heights in their Mitzvah work — far beyond their wildest dreams.

These three statements might sound very threatening to the multitudes of people doing their own private Tzedakah work or working for Mitzvah organizations. On the surface, the General Rule and its Corollaries would imply that whatever the "conventional" Mitzvah person is doing is insufficient. This is not my purpose in developing The Rule and Corollaries. I am simply stating that the Mitzvah Heroes are pre-eminent in their field of endeavor (in this case, Mitzvahs), as Einstein and Newton were in Physics, Beethoven and Mozart in music, Shakespeare and Dante in literature, and Rembrandt, da Vinci, and Michelangelo in art.

And just as a physicist or musician or writer or painter would yearn to learn from the Distinguished Ones, so, too, for Mitzvah work. The Mitzvah-Hero-"conventional"-Mitzvah-worker relationship is analogous.

The Grand Opportunity presents itself to all of us: to attach ourselves to the Mitzvah Heroes, to learn from them, adopt their techniques, and attempt to integrate the finest aspects of their personalities into our own. This does not happen very frequently, and I think there are two critical reasons why: (1) The General Rule and Corollaries *appear to* undercut the meaning of professionalism. Training long years to master the field (psychology, medicine, social work, community planning, sociology, hospital administration, etc.), the degree recipient expects a certain status-recognition. I can understand that very well. I have been a writer for 20 years now and have fought hard to gain some recognition as a serious poet and prose writer. Jealousy, anger, frustration, and insecurity ruled the "early years of struggle", and I lost perspective of my purpose as a writer. Any other writer's or poet's successes undercut my own and slashed away at my self-image. I was — in my own eyes — not good enough, or, at best, not very good. So I understand why professionals might feel threatened by my recommendation to "walk in the footsteps of the Mitzvah Heroes". But the presence of Mitzvah Heroes ought to be seen as an opportunity, not a threat.

(2, i.e., the second reason why not-so-many people take the step of meeting, learning from, and working with the Mitzvah Heroes): There is a serious misunderstanding about the exact nature of the Mitzvah Heroes on the part of "conventionals" and "professionals". Many people would agree that the Mitzvah Heroes are sincere, goodhearted people, but naive about the reality of human needs. This is definitely not the case. I have referred to the Mitzvah Heroes as pre-eminent in their field, as distinguished as the Einsteins and Michelangelos in their separate fields of accomplishment. They are most certainly *not* naive; they are *not* uninformed, and they are not living in Some Other World, soaked in Unreal Idealism. (Some benignly view them as Good Souls, but, at best, only capable of bumbling their way through.) To the contrary, they have a most profound and — for lack of a better term — true grasp of reality.

When the "conventional" or "professional" surrenders his or her fears, insecurities, and anger and allows himself or herself to be dazzled and inspired, the results are always the same: greater benefits for those who desperately need their talents.

Take for example the late Irene Gaster of Jerusalem: a Giant. She single-handedly touched the lives of hundreds of retarded individuals, and their families. As others recognized her unique talents, they came to her for guidance. The most expert professionals in the field consulted and often deferred to her wisdom.

Take Myriam Mendilow and the sum total of those who have learned from her, the ones in the United States and Canada and throughout Europe and in Australia and many other countries, Mendilow's students who have profoundly changed the lives of elderly people because of her insight and actions.

Dresses made at the Yad Ezrah
sewing workshop.

Take any of the people in this book: Hadassah Levi, Janet Marchese, Uri Lupoliansky, Reb Osher Freund, of course....

Take, for example, The First Person in the World who decided that pets or computers in old age homes would open up lives that were in disastrous decline, would add days, weeks, months, years to elderly people who wanted to die just because there was no meaningful connection left with society. (Pet/Computer Formula: 3 more animals or machines Minus 2 nurses = same or more longevity.)

Take the quiet Mitzvah Heroes in your own community, doing their exquisite work without fanfare and news cameras rolling.

And that is why Reb Osher's Ohr Yerushalayim is my very favorite aspect of Yad Ezrah.

When I am in Jerusalem for the summer, I usually go to synagogue in the Yemin Moshe neighborhood. It is a nice service, pleasant, and when you stand up for some of the prayers, you can look out the window and see the walls of the Old City. The man who reads from the Torah reads with great enthusiasm. Even the food afterwards is abundant and tasty.

But more than that, I think this synagogue has an extra element of holiness to it. During the week, this is where Yad Ezrah teaches Torah to many people who had been on the fringes of society: mentally ill people, people with lesser or greater psychological and emotional difficulties, retarded individuals, and some people in-definable other than to call them outcasts. No one is an outcast at Ohr Yerusha-layim. They are taken in and offered Reb Osher's very special kind of Torah, a teaching of gentleness, love, and understanding. I know the man who runs the Yeshiva....He is there Shabbat morning, and he has the same look of The Gentle-ness of Mitzvahs on his face, the look I recognize from Reb Osher's own appear-ance. Looking at the man as I had first looked at Reb Osher, I knew that during the week miracles were happening in this place.

I rarely speak of Holiness. Holiness seems so overwhelming...but, it would seem to me that Reb Osher is a holy person, though he might humbly deny it. I would defer, then, to his humility and say that his work is holy work, and those who have shared in his Mitzvah activities sparkle with a touch of holiness.

Reb Osher Freund, c/o Yad Ezrah, 15 HaRav Sorotzkin St., POB 7199, Jerusalem, 526-133.

RABBI LEIB HEBER

When I first met Rabbi Leib Heber, it occurred to me that he *looked like* what most people think a Tzaddik is supposed to look like: he had a white beard and a saintly aura about him. He was a learned man, and for all his learning, he was never arrogant. His humility struck you from the first moment of encounter.

As with so many Mitzvah heroes, Rabbi Heber was involved in many kinds of Mitzvahs but specialized in one in particular: he visited Jews in mental institu-tions throughout Western Pennsylvania. When I met him he was vigorous, *very* sharp, and nearly 80 years old. On one occasion I found that I had been guilty of talking down to him — we do that sometimes with elderly people. I was shocked at myself for doing it, corrected it, and never heard a word of rebuke from him. Rabbi Heber turned the conversation around and upward with a bit of humor. It woke me up.

I would imagine it takes an enormously strong constitution to go in and out of institutions...even as a visitor. It can take a very heavy toll on you, draining your physical and psychological energies. Institutions are not at all like the outside world. But for years Rabbi Heber was in and out of them and back again and yet again, bringing food and joy and holidays and birthdays to his people, or, as he called them, His Children. Only this: he was a father to them but he was never an-gry at them, for he was a very gentle man.

Rabbi Heber brought Judaism to the Jews in the wards, often something hard to come by in a secular institution. He reminded them of their place in God's plan as seen by Jewish tradition; he lifted their souls. They, no less than anyone else, were entitled to understand the Torah, Rabbi Heber's very soothing kind of Torah.

At one time I think he and his driver were making the rounds to 18 different institutions in Pittsburgh and throughout a wide geographic area. That is quite a circuit, but the adults and children he visited depended on him. As I have asked before with other Mitzvah heroes, how many hundreds of people did he reach and touch in those years?

His message was that mentally ill people (tortured of mind as they might be) were still and always people. The same was true for mentally retarded individuals (slower or lower-functioning, perhaps, than other people) they were still, and always, human beings, all made in God's image. He knew that from the Bible and Talmud, and he embodied those principles. Few have taught so well the essence of being human, both in the way they are as human beings and how they ought to treat other human beings. A precious few.

In a very real way, Rabbi Heber reminded us who knew him of another Tzaddik from a couple of decades ago, Reb Arye Levin of Jerusalem. Both had a gentle touch, and both projected the sense that no matter who you were, you were important to them, to all people, and to God. Reb Arye, as he was known, spent his time with prisoners — even the most hardened criminals; Rabbi Heber, with those whose minds were not defined by society as "normal".

Rabbi Heber passed away about a year ago. In Hebrew, there are three essential terms applied to someone's passing: "Met", which just means "died", "Niftar", which is a nicer term, more polite, meaning "taken leave of, departed", and "Nistalek", which is reserved only for a saintly few. "Nistalek" carries connotations of being "removed", "taken back", as if Heaven wanted to reclaim a most precious soul. That is why "Nistalek" is the most appropriate word for Rabbi Heber's passing, for his was a most precious soul.

Western Pennsylvania Auxiliary for Exceptional People, 281 Sharon Dr., Pittsburgh, PA 15221, 412-271-1578. They are carrying on Rabbi Heber's work.

THE MYSTERY MAN WITH THE $100 BILL

Every year the Council of Jewish Federations holds its annual convention, the General Assembly. It is a gathering of thousands of professionals and volunteers from around the continent, people devoted to raising hundreds of millions of dollars for local Jewish projects, for Israel, and for Jewish communities around the world.

Once, I think it was about three or four years ago, when the convention was in Atlanta, I was standing in the lobby of the hotel talking with some friends. A man briefly interrupted our conversation, saying something like, "One of my relatives heard you give a talk, so here is something for your Tzedakah work..." He put a crumpled bill in my hands and faded into the crowd. My partners-in-conversation had that look on their faces, something like, "How in the world did you do that?" I must have mumbled something like, "Nothing to it."

I put the bill in my pocket, took it out later on, and saw that it was a $100 bill.

For the past three years I have been teaching at the General Assembly at what is called the Lunch and Learn. Every year I mention The Mystery Man With The $100 Bill. And every year, when the session is over and people are standing around me buying some of my books, he appears, puts a bill into my hands, and then fades into the crowd. Every year it is $100.

I think I have found out who the man is; I'm almost certain. But I can't tell you.

II. PEOPLE I STILL HAVE TO MEET

THE PEOPLE OF NORTH PLATTE, NEBRASKA
(I owe this one to Charles Kuralt)

I have the 1985 Rand McNally Road Atlas spread out in front of me, a gift from my auto insurance agent. I have turned to Nebraska, and the state stretches across two pages from Iowa and Missouri on the East to Wyoming and Colorado on the West, South Dakota above and Kansas below.

I have been looking for Elk Creek, Buffalo Grove, Maxwell, Dry Valley, Arcadia, and Brady, but they are too small to be on the map. I *did* manage to find Lodgepole and Big Springs (no population figures listed in the index; too small), and Hershey (pop. 633), Stromsburg (1,290), Atkinson (1521), Ogallala (5,638 souls) and Ansley (644). Somewhere near a geographical center is North Platte (24,479), but Stromsburg is over 150 miles away as the crow flies, and some of the other towns are not that much closer. I just know I've been through North Platte sometime, perhaps driving back from the West Coast on a cross-country trip. Interstate 80 goes right by it, across the North Platte River. I'm sure I must have stopped there because it was the only town of any size between Cheyenne and Lincoln. I must have stopped there, at least for coffee and to stretch my legs before doing the long drive of four or five hours to Lincoln and Omaha.

Now I want to go back. I want to meet some of the North Platte folks, and the people of these other towns...some of which are too small and "insignificant" to make it on to the Rand McNally map. I *have* to go back. Charles Kuralt urges me to do so, and if there's anyone who can find Mitzvah Heroes in the most out-of-the-way places, it's Charles Kuralt. He goes by another kind of map.

In his book, *On the Road with Charles Kuralt*, he tells a story from World War II. The fact was, that between 1942 and 1945 millions of soldiers passed through North Platte on troop trains, going east and west to fight in the war. The trains came through every day with as many as 10,000 soldiers in a single day.

What happened out there in the middle of nowhere was that the people of North Platte and all those little towns far from anything but fields upon fields of food growing for our tables — these people fed every one of the soldiers passing through North Platte. Charles Kuralt understandably finds it hard to believe, and asks, "...what happened when you ran out of food?" — to which Jessie Hutchens, one of those who stood there feeding the soldiers replied, "We didn't!" Sandwiches, meat, fruit, pies, coffee, warmth, hugs, love, everything.

I'll need a lot of time for this trip. Over 120 towns took part. That's a lot of driving around, but if I manage to get to four or five of the places, including North Platte, of course, who knows what I will learn about Mitzvahs?

BOB GELDOF

Until a couple of years ago, Bob Geldof was not the kind of person you would have wanted to come over for dinner and hang out with your kids. You (and I) probably had never heard of him, though young people knew him as the leader of a rock group, The Boomtown Rats. I was told on good authority that he used to release live rats into the audience during his concerts. Now I'm *sure* you wouldn't have wanted him to come over for dinner. And I'm *sure* you wouldn't have wanted him to hang out with your kids.

But he's not just Bob Geldof anymore, he's *Sir* Bob Geldof, a Knight of the British Empire, complete with ceremony, Queen Elizabeth, the whole works...at the ripe age of 35. That's because he organized Live Aid, the 15-hour marathon concert to raise money for people starving in Africa. Those who know these kinds of things estimate that the worldwide satellite hook-up brought the British concert to 1,500,000,000 people (that's 1.5 *billion* people) in 100 different countries. And then there was Band Aid in the United States, another mammoth concert. The money raised came to $120,000,000, according to an article in *The Boston Globe*.

That's almost too much to absorb at one time. The numbers are too big when you consider that the concerts were organized by a kid who had a tough upbringing on the outskirts of Dublin and wound up letting rats loose in auditoriums full of people. The facts are so remote from each other, worlds apart.

But the story is really very simple. Geldof had seen on television the starving faces and swollen bellies of Ethiopian children. We all had seen those pictures, most recently the Ethiopians, and in the not-too-distant-past, the Biafrans and Cambodians. This is how he articulated his reaction to one interviewer: "When I saw the television footage of the starving, I felt anger, shame and outrage....Hunger is a crime. I thought of myself as an accomplice. I knew a crime was occurring and I was doing nothing about it."

Geldof felt a wave of shame. The rock star wanted to do something, something to shift some of the world's surplus food lying around in warehouses and get it to starving people in Africa. In the interview he continues, "I decided to utilize my abilities to help. *I knew people.* [Italics mine.] I thought I could do something to help and then bow out." He hit a sensitive nerve with the full range of people in the music and entertainment industry. Live Aid grew and grew, and Geldof admits that, had he thought about how big the project would grow, he wouldn't have done it.

Simon and Garfunkel had 500,000 people at their concert in Central Park.

Elvis had hook-ups that tied in millions.

But this was a billion and a half people.

Because he *knew people* and he and those people could make things happen once they applied themselves to the Mitzvah.

Since then, Sir Bob Geldof has even met Mother Teresa...and he has argued with her. They disagree about suffering. According to Geldof, she understands suffering as a test. She argued that pain was cleansing. Geldof replied: Pain is not cleansing. Pain is pain.

Two Catholics, a rock-star-become-Knight and a nun-become-Nobel-Prize-Laureate, arguing theology. It must have been a strange scene, but no one would question his right to argue. He's had experience.

With Live Aid and Band Aid behind him, he can think of other things than just being a rock star. He says, "Fame is liberating. I have a platform. I can do other things, go beyond music."

In Jewish terms that's Power=Mitzvah power.

RANYA KELLY - THE BAG LADY OF ARVADA

Ranya Kelly, young, comfortable, middle-class, found 500 pairs of shoes in a dumpster. She had driven from her home to a small shopping mall to try to find a box she needed. Rummaging through the dumpster, she found the shoes.

This is a painful and difficult story, a story of callousness and vindictiveness, but with a happy ending. Stick with it.

Even though the story has such a strange beginning, Kelly's time in and around dumpsters has paid off. Her first dumpster was near a shoe store in Arvada, CO, a suburb of Denver. At first her friends jokingly called her "the bag lady of Arvada", but they don't laugh any more. They admire her.

All those shoes Ranya Kelly found were new — only they had a little yellow paint on them. When she took them home, she took the paint off with a little paint thinner and started giving the shoes away to family and friends. But there were too many shoes....so she called some places that work with poor people, and that's where the story *really* begins.

One of the shelters welcomed Kelly's donation, and when she got down there, she was shocked at what poverty looked like face-to-face. She decided then and there to go back to that First Dumpster on a more regular basis. The dumpster was right near a shoe store, and she always found a few pairs of shoes. Then she would clean them up and take them down to the shelter. Simple enough.

Then Kelly broadened her range, visiting other dumpsters near shoe stores, but these stores apparently cut the shoes up before throwing them away. So back she went to her First Dumpster in Arvada. She hit pay dirt again and found hundreds of other pairs of shoes.

Then came the fateful step: Kelly called the company's local office in Denver and asked why some of their stores would intentionally destroy the shoes rather than donate them to organizations that could get them to needy people. And then came the fateful reply — that it was the company's policy to throw them away (shoes worn and returned, slightly damaged shoes, some other nameless categories of shoes) so that people would not come back and ask for cash or credit.

I've read this article again and again, and I still can't figure out why people coming in with shoes like these — without a receipt — would get cash or credit anyway. I assume that most business establishments, at least as far as my experience goes, refuse to refund or give credit without a receipt. So something doesn't make sense.

But to continue: one day Kelly was caught in the act by one of the employees. Her cover was blown, and she pleaded with the salesperson not to tell the Boss. Soon, however, the shoes in her First Dumpster were thrown away — this time sliced up.

The plot thickens: The Bag Lady of Arvada called the shoe store's central headquarters in Kansas, asking the higher-ups why they had this policy. She got the same inexplicable answer....they didn't want returns for cash or credit. When she suggested that they simply mark the shoes with indelible ink, they asked for her name and address.

I feel like stopping, as I did when I first read the article, and asking, "Hey, fellas, what's going on here? Are you really saying this with a straight face? Name and address? Is this the CIA or something?" And they told her to stay out of their trash; it belonged to them. If she persisted, there would be problems for her: they'd have her arrested.

I feel like stopping, as I did when I read the article a second and third time and asking, "Hey, fellas, what's going on here? Are you serious? Is the House Un-American Activities Committee still alive and well in the Midwest?"

I promised a happy ending....Kelly checked with the police, and they said, no, it wasn't the shoe stores' property once it was put in the dumpster. It belonged to the trash collection people, and when Kelly called *them*, they were more than happy to let her take whatever she found, as long as she didn't scatter junk all over the place.

Knowledge and facts in hand, Kelly started making the rounds of other dumpsters and picking out perfectly good items which she took down to shelters, including mattresses and furniture and blankets. As she got more skilled at her rather off-odor labor of love, she heard other excuses from various merchants, including something about tax write-offs. She called a number of accountants and even the IRS about that one, and found out their answers simply weren't true. Her conclusion was: it was too much trouble for the merchants to donate the goods to charities — as valid an excuse as possible for busy business people. She would allow them that. But these other lines, the threats?

Even when Kelly volunteered to pick up the merchandise and deliver it for them, many companies refused. Now that's just plain mean.

Then, after Kelly made some other inquiries, and after some more pushing, company policy began to change. The shoe store chain whose dumpster she had first visited gave in. Fifty of their stores in the Denver area would turn over the shoes to her for distribution. They would even box them up nicely for her. And the company added that, if the project works out well in Denver, they could very well expand it into the 40-some other States they cover where they had other outlets.

That's a lot of thousands of pairs of shoes for lots of thousands of people who don't have decent shoes.

Free.

Victory! (Now call her to start your own shoe project: 303-431-0904.)

MITZVAH HEROES IN THE WORLD OF SPORTS (by Garth Potts)

Somewhere in my consciousness there is a 10-year-old boy who collects baseball cards and idolizes sports heroes and truly wants them to be special. I now have three little boys and a girl of my own with whom I would like to share some of those special growing-up memories as well.

My personal bubble was burst when I met some of these "heroes" up close and discovered their clay feet and enlarged egos. While it is not fair to paint an entire profession with such a broad brush, my perception is that, in terms of comprehending the true meaning of Tzedakah, this group is somewhat of a washout. What frustrates me is the wasted opportunities. By virtue of many athletes' position, finances, access to media, and public adulation, they have a tremendous chance not only to do, but also to teach and influence others so profoundly by their actions. I can only guess what could be done if the same class, status, and power were conferred on Tzaddikim.

Nonetheless, a few examples of fine Mitzvah work have emerged from this group of highly-paid, compensation-deferred, long-term-contracted athletes. *Sports Illustrated* recently highlighted several athletes as their Sportsmen and Sportswomen of the Year. Their efforts are outstanding models for all.

I remember the quiet dignity of Kenyan Kip Keino winning the 1500 meters in the 1968 Mexico City Olympiad. Keino bested those who came to compete that day, and yet all of the superior training available in the developed world could not overcome the grit and courage of the performance of this talented runner from Kenya. Kip Keino performs on a different stage these days. Now 47 years old, he and his wife, Phyllis, manage a farm and a sporting goods business back in their homeland. Throughout their married lives they have taken in over 100 orphans from all over the tortured lands of Kenya and Uganda. These children are malnourished, malformed, maltreated, abandoned, but none of these disadvantages matters to the Keinos. Their income is sufficient but not extravagant, and the lessons taught by the way they live their lives are lessons of love and self-respect. (And I complain sometimes about trying to raise 4 kids!)

To give other examples: Dave Winfield is the well-known outfielder with the Yankees who demanded that Designated Owner George Steinbrenner include funding for his foundation for children in his multi-million dollar contract. That model suggested an idea to point guard Rory Sparrow of the Chicago Bulls. Starting with the goals of education, jobs, and summer recreation, blended with drug and nutrition counseling, his own Rory Sparrow Foundation has flourished. He returned to his inner-city roots to live near the hundreds of participants in his programs in Paterson, NJ, and New York City, and has been an active role model for these kids during the last 6 years.

Winston-Salem, NC, has its own version of the 100 Neediest Families who provide the charitable focus at Christmastime. The difference in that city, though, is that an obscure Wake Forest senior running back named Chip Rives plays Santa Claus in lieu of a citywide drive. For the past two years, Rives has raised sufficient funds to buy new toys for children who rarely have anything new. Chip Rives is nothing special as an athlete. He's just a person.

I lived and died for the Buffalo Sabres from the mid-70's to now. Among the team's nemeses (and there were unfortunately many of them) were the New York Islanders who boasted about a certain gutsy player named Bob Bourne. Tough on the ice, he is remarkably tender at home since the birth of his son, who is disabled with spina bifida. Besides the special attention and love they give their child, Bourne and his wife have devoted their efforts to raising consciousness about and funds for people involved in fighting this disease. More important, their own lesson about Tzedakah has extended to other causes in which they have become involved, such as services for unwed mothers. Their Mitzvah work grows.

It is easy for so many well-heeled athletes to write checks for several figures, drop them in the mail, and then forget about whom the money might benefit. Not so Patty Sheehan, one of the top LPGA golfers on the tour. The girls at the Tigh Sheehan group home in California are beneficiaries of both Patty's time and money. Her adult role model is an important part of Patty's visits, but the simple fact of her taking time out of the golf tour (and her livelihood) is even more significant.

The list continues with Dale Murphy of the Atlanta Braves and his work for cystic fibrosis. 400-meter U.S. record holder Judi Brown King's volunteer work at an Oregon Relief Nursery is another example. Furthermore, Leigh Steinberg, a well-known sports agent insists that all his clients contract for a certain percentage of their income to be "returned" to their universities or home communities. Babe Ruth even visited sick kids in hospitals and once "promised" to hit a home run for one of them.

I suppose it's unfair to have unusual expectations of people who have unique physical gifts and opportunities. Yet, is it any less excusable for such people to waste those opportunities on frivolous pleasures (and sometimes somewhat dangerous ones at that)? Apparently the maturity and wisdom we expect of ourselves to be a Mensch all-too-frequently falls on deaf ears in the upper echelons of sport. Still, there are these few individuals who persevere (and some others I have not mentioned) — special people swimming upstream against the current. They set an example of Menschlichkeit in strong contrast to the stories of drug and alcohol excesses, greed and violence on and off the field. They clearly demonstrate that sports heroes can, indeed, become Mitzvah heroes if they but avail themselves of the opportunity. Particularly because of the many pressures just to bask (or wallow) in their fame, we ought to admire them that much more for what they accomplish.

AND WILLIAM MARRIOTT

Chief Executive Officer of the Marriott Hotels chain, whose company's policy states that 5% of the workforce must be developmentally disabled people.

AND BEN AND JERRY

of Ben and Jerry's Ice Cream, who give away 7 1/2% of their pre-tax profits to Tzedakah, and who (rumor has it) have a rule that no one at their company makes more than 4 or 5 times as much as the lowest-paid employee.

AND EUGENE LANG

who promised a 6th-grade class that if, they stayed in school and graduated the 12th grade he would pay for their college education. And I also want to meet all the other people in other cities who are doing the same, following Lang's lead. (I already know one of them, Charlotte Kramer, in Cleveland.)

AND MR. ESCALANTE

(or so he is called in the movie "Stand and Deliver"), the real-live teacher in the East Los Angeles school who taught math to a bunch of Mexican-American highschool students who had everything going against them. Escalante took them to new heights — advanced placement calculus exams. He taught them that dishing out chicken in a fast-food restaurant was not their only hope.

AND ANN MEDLOCK

who has this thing called The Giraffe Project (45 W. 45th St., #402, New York, NY 10035, 800-344-TALL). "Giraffes" are people who stick their necks out...to do the right thing. She searches the media and the country looking for Mitzvah heroes.

AND CHARLES KURALT

who could keep me going for many more years, just by putting pins in a map of the United States, and telling me, "Here is Ms. X, who does the most amazing things....Over there, in Nevada, about 45 miles Northeast of Reno is Mr. Y, who does..."

REFLECTIONS XI

For a long time now I have thought about organizing a convention of Mitzvah heroes.

The closest I have come to seeing something like that was at the Conference on Alternatives in Jewish Education (CAJE) annual conference in the summer of 1986 at the University of Maryland. Inspiring people from well over a dozen outstanding Mitzvah projects were brought in, including some from Israel such as Uri Lupoliansky, Myriam Mendilow, and Hadassah Levi. Others I have written about in this book were there. On one particular evening, the more than 2,000 conference attendees split up into groups, to listen to and interact with each of the specific heroes.

It was a wonderful evening, magnificent.

Still, this is not exactly what I have in mind for my convention. I would like to bring in about 15 or 20 of the heroes and leave them to themselves for a couple of days, just so they can meet each other and talk about whatever they would want to talk about. Then I would probably let in a few Students of Mitzvah Heroes. (I would insist on being one of them, of course.)

I'd leave them alone, too...no media coverage, no glitz. I would want them just to talk and talk and teach other, ask questions, plan things, share each other's visions. No one would deliver speeches or papers. I would just let them be.

Whether or not they would come up with some statement or program to solve All the Problems of the World, I can't say.

I'll have to wait until the convention happens.

POSTSCRIPT: THE HONORARY INMATE

Where to begin?

Kimberly Martin is 10 years old and has leukemia. A prisoner at the Missouri Eastern Correctional Center saw an article about how the family couldn't afford to pay for all of her treatments. The prisoner decided to do something about it.

Since then, the prisoners have sent in $25,580.27 to help pay for anything that can help keep her alive.

And Kimberly — the Honorary Inmate — visits her friends at the maximum security prison. (She even has an Honorary Inmate ID.)

When I first saw this article, I pictured some easy-going minimum security prison for white-collar prisoners, rich people caught cheating on the IRS or embezzling from their partners. Not so: these prisoners are serving long sentences for serious felonies...including 1st degree murder.

And when I first saw the article, I thought Kimberly went to the prison just once — to thank the men. Not so: she visits regularly, including on her birthday, which was appropriately named by the prisoners "Kimberly Martin Day".

One prisoner admits that, at first, they did it just to get back at the people who run the prison. They don't much like being told what to do, and they thought the administration would give them a hard time. It was a small-scale rebellion.

The warden and his staff didn't object, Kimberly was invited to visit, and, instead of just saying, "Hi!" and "Thank you" and then leaving, she and the inmates spent hours together playing ball and talking.

More than once the doctors gave Kimberly only a few days to live. The article in *Parade Magazine* is from February. It's now May, and I can't find anywhere what the latest prognosis is.

Jewish tradition says there are not only miracles in this world but also miracles within miracles. This is a story of miracles within miracles.

And I would like to know if the friendship of the Felons and the Little Kid is overriding everything the medical profession could possibly predict.

Wondrous things these Mitzvahs....

Glossary

(H=Hebrew; Y=Yiddish)

Alef (H): the first letter of the Hebrew alphabet. Alef-Bet=the alphabet.

Aliya (H): literally "going up". "Making Aliya" = moving to Israel. (Israel was considered higher than all other countries.

Chassidic (H): referring to a Jewish religious movement founded in Eastern Europe in the 18th century by the Baal Shem Tov. Chassidism is known for its sense of joy and ecstasy, particularly manifested in prayer, song, and dance.

Chevra (h): any group; a group of friends.

Hachnassat Kallah (H): the Mitzvah of providing for poor brides and couple about to be married.

Halbashat HaKallah (H): Literally "dressing the bride". The Yemenite ceremony of dressing the bride in the traditional outfit.

HaShem (H): God.

Kallah (H): a bride.

Kavod (H): dignity, respect.

Knesset (H): The Israeli Parliament.

Matzah (H): unleavened bread eaten on Passover.

Mazon (H): food, also a Jewish organization that raises funds to feed people. (MAZON — A Jewish Response to Hunger.)

Menorot (H-pl.; sing.-Menorah): a 9-branched candle holder for the holiday of Hanukkah.

Mensch (Y; adj.-Menschlich; abs.-Menschlichkeit): an upright, responsible, decent, caring, compassionate person.

Mezuzot (H-pl.; sing.-Mezuzah): a small container holding an inscription from the Torah that is hung on the doorposts of Jewish houses, according to instructions in Deuteronomy Chapter 6.

Midrash (H):Jewish literature from the first 7 or 8 centuries of the Common Era containing stories, aphorisms, and narratives. Also, any non-legal portion of the Talmud. Also used to refer to a specific story or tale.

Mitzvah (H): literally "commandment" or "instruction" — good deeds done by people according to the prescriptions of traditional Jewish texts, such as visiting the sick, comforting mourners, and giving Tzedakah. In this book, Mitzvah is usually synonymous with Tzedakah. (See chapter called "Terminology" at beginning of book.)

Purim (H): Jewish holiday celebrating the victory of the Jews of Persia over the wicked Haman. The holiday is celebrated with great joy, dancing, parades, masks, and merrymaking.

Rabbanit (H): a Rabbi's wife.
Rebbetzin (Y): a Rabbi's wife.

Shabbat (H): the Sabbath.
Shoah (H): the Holocaust.
Simcha (H): joy, a joyous occasion.

Talitot (H-pl.; sing.-Talit): a shawl-like garment with ritual fringes (Tzitzit) on the four corners, worn by Jews during morning prayers.

Talmud (H): an immense compendium of discussions, tales, aphorisms, legal give-and-take, and insights about Judaism, developed in Jewish academies (Yeshivas) during the first five centuries of the Common Era.

Tam, Tamim (H; abstract-Temimut): innocent, pure, straightforward, simple, naive the last two — in the positive sense of the term).

Tikkun (H): fixing up, repairing. Tikkun Olam=repairing the world.

Torah (H): literally "teaching". Originally meaning the Five Books of Moses, expanded to include the entirety of Jewish study and learning. "To talk Torah" is to discuss these texts.

Tov (H): good.

Tzaddik (H): a Righteous Person.

Tzadeket (H): a Righteous Woman.

Tzedakah (H): the distinctly Jewish method of performing charitable acts. From the word "Tzedek", Justice. (see "Terminology" chapter at beginning of book.)

Tzedek(H): Justice. (See "Terminology" chapter at beginning of book.)

Yarmulka (Y): a small, round head covering worn by religious Jews.
Yiddishkeit: Judaism.

Zaken (H): an old person, an Elder.
Ziv (H): radiance.

DANNY SIEGEL is a free-lance author, poet, and lecturer who resides in Rockville, Maryland, when not on his speaking tours or in Israel distributing Tzedakah monies. He is the author of five books of poetry, four of which are now out of print, as well as three anthologies of his selected writings.

Danny is the author of a book of essays and three anthologies on the subject of Midrash and Halachah, now combined into a single volume. He is also co-author with Allan Gould of a book of Jewish humor, and tapes of his poetry readings and humor presentations have been produced.

The publication of *Gym Shoes and Irises. Book Two,* rounded out Danny's devotion to the "how-to" of personalized Tzedakah begun many years before the issuance of the first *Gym Shoes and Irises* in 1982. His new volume: *Munbaz II and Other Mitzvah Heroes* is another major contribution by Danny Siegel in recognizing the deeds of loving-kindness by the good people of this world.

Siegel is a popular lecturer at synagogues, Jewish federations, community centers, conventions, and retreats, where he teaches Tzedakah and Jewish values and recites from his works. His books and talks have received considerable acclaim throughout the entire North American Jewish community.